JUSTICE.

MERCY.

HUMILITY.

A Simple Path to Following JESUS

Rusty George

BETHANYHOUSE
a division of Baker Publishing Group
www.BethanyHouse.com

Published by Bethany House Publishers
11400 Hampshire Avenue South
Bloomington, Minnesota 55438
www.bethanyhouse.com

Bethany House Publishers is a division of
Baker Publishing Group, Grand Rapids, Michigan

Printed in the United States of America

ISBN 978-0-7642-3080-6

Library of Congress Control Number: 2018038555

Cover design by Dan Pitts
Author represented by Don Gates from The Gates Group

19 20 21 22 23 24 25   7 6 5 4 3 2 1

"In unpacking this gem of a verse—Micah 6:8—Rusty manages to be wise, insightful, and even laugh-out-loud funny. What a powerful resource for those who want to bring focus to their faith."

—Christine Caine, founder,
The A21 Campaign and Propel Women

"It's hard to think of three qualities that are more needed—by the church or in our country or in the world—than these three. May Rusty's book not only get widely read, may it get deeply realized."

—John Ortberg, pastor, Menlo Church

"This is a quiet book, which is, of course, always the most dangerous. There is breathing room and freedom in its pages, much like in Micah 6:8, the verse the book is based on. The simplicity of justice, mercy, and humility follows verses that heap more work upon us to please God. . . . Thousands of rams, ten thousand rivers of oil, my firstborn child . . . what will please God? The response is the whisper of these three words, and Rusty invites us to linger and rest in them. Your soul probably needs this book . . . mine did."

—Nancy Ortberg, CEO of Transforming the Bay with Christ

"One of the best parts of reading this book is knowing Rusty personally and watching him live this message out. *Justice. Mercy. Humility.* is a quick and necessary message that I need to hear over and over. If you aim to become more like Jesus, this book is worth the read."

—Carey Nieuwhof, founding pastor,
Connexus Church, Ontario, Canada

For Lorrie.

No one has modeled Micah 6:8
more for me than you.

Contents

Step 4: Walk Humbly.

one

Why Is This So Complicated?

Ads for pharmaceutical products can be both entertaining and horrifying. The disclaimers for all the possible side effects are often longer than the explanation of the benefits of the drug. This is what we often refer to as the fine print.

May cause anxiety, depression, an itch on your back you can't reach, fear of clowns, running with scissors, barking at the moon, and an unhealthy obsession with fire.

Obviously, I'm exaggerating, but still. When did drugs intended to help anxiety start inducing anxiety? And more than that, when did commercials for anxiety drugs start making me practically need anxiety medicine? When did the fine print get so long?

Ever feel like the call to follow Jesus comes with some fine print?

If someone were to ask you, "So all I have to do is believe?" wouldn't there be a part of you that pauses and thinks, *Well, yes . . . but . . .* And here comes the list. For me, this list is what I've grown up with, what I've spent my life telling others to do, and is just part of life. But for others, it's fine print.

This is what makes some of us reluctant to share our faith in the first place. We know we have a great message to share—"Jesus loves you and has a wonderful plan for your life. He offers forgiveness, salvation, and eternal life. All you have to do is believe." But it's the fine print that seemingly holds us back.

Yes, believe in Jesus, but also . . .

love others, forgive those who hurt you, pray for those who persecute you, have joy, be patient, stay faithful, be gentle with your words, give to the hurting, tithe, live in peace, serve in your church, be kind to everyone on the freeway, go to church every week, read your Bible every day, pray without ceasing, don't drink, don't smoke, don't chew tobacco, don't go with girls that do, and confess your sins every night, for if you don't you might wake up in hell. God bless!

Why do we do this?

I think we don't know what to do with all the things in the Bible that seem to be necessary, so we make them into a to-do list. Then we treat them as the way we get God's attention and favor.

For centuries we've been trying to figure out how to get God's attention. And not only get his attention, but gain his approval. It has driven some to exhaustion, others to disbelief, and some nearly mad. Is this really what Jesus intended when he said, "Follow me"? Is this what God had in mind when he said, "You will be my people and I will be your God"?

Sometimes people do seemingly crazy things to live out the fine print.

I had just completed what seemed like a typical day at the office, and I was heading outside to begin my short drive home when I heard an awful noise across the parking lot. It sounded like a trumpet, and the only thing that kept me from looking for the return of Christ was that I assumed Gabriel would play better than what I was hearing. I scanned the area and saw an old Pontiac circling our lot with a passenger hanging out the window blowing a trumpet.

Apparently I stood stunned long enough to catch their attention. Once we locked eyes, they seemed intent on chasing me down. The car barreled up to the sidewalk and came to a screeching halt. The driver and the passenger bounded out of the car and headed over to me. Just before I got into the Karate Kid stance to defend myself, the trumpeter asked, "Are you the lead pastor?" Several responses came to my mind, the first being, "No." Of course, this would be a lie, but doesn't the end justify the means? I also thought about referring him to another pastor, hoping that would distract him. Instead, I went with the truth. "Yes," I said hesitantly.

Once I correctly identified myself, they were resolute on their mission: to pray a blessing on this church and its pastor. I admit I need prayer as much as the next guy, so I gladly received it. However, once the prayer began, one of the gentlemen left the holy huddle and went back to the car for something. After he returned, he began to anoint me, pouring oil he had just retrieved on my head and hands while the other prayed for me. I'm not sure what he said. He might have prayed for me to turn into a chicken for all I know, but I do know I'll never forget the experience.

What causes someone to do this? Why did this manner of prayer and worship captivate these guys? What persuaded them to drive around a parking lot blowing a trumpet over a church and then anointing and praying for its pastor?

It is probably the same thing that has caused me to get up at three in the morning and put a suit on.

I was in Bible college and was resolute in my passion to know God and be found faithful in his presence. My roommate and I had heard about one of the professors who had a daily practice of getting up at three in the morning, showering, shaving, and putting on a suit to meet with God. He did this every day. So one day we decided to give it a try. After all, the professor was a devout man of God who had all the indications of Christ being fully formed in him.

We set our alarms for three and laid out our suits, giddy with anticipation. One factor we'd failed to consider was that, since we were college students, we usually stayed up past midnight. We tried to go to bed earlier, but we just couldn't sleep. No sooner had we finally dozed off than our alarm clock sounded. That didn't discourage us, though. We bounded out of our beds and showered, shaved, and suited up for our meeting with God. Then we grabbed our Bibles, notebooks, pens, flashlights, and a couple of lawn chairs and went out to a nearby hillside to set up our makeshift prayer cloister.

I was expecting the heavens to part and a bright light to shine down on us to welcome our presence. Instead, after we prayed, read, and journaled, we both just fell asleep in the chairs.

Did we get through to God? If he said something to us, we were too asleep to hear.

People Have Always Strived for God's Attention

You may not blow a trumpet or put on a suit at three in the morning, but all of us have our routines. Perhaps you go to church. You may like it, you may not, but something inside of you probably thinks, *If I go, I'll get in good with God. If I don't, then I shouldn't bother asking for anything this week.*

Maybe it's Bible reading and prayer. You have a Bible filled with highlights and notes in the margins. You keep a prayer journal, and though you are faithful to this time of reading and reflection, inside you secretly wonder if that is enough. *Am I doing it right? Why does it seem some of my prayers aren't getting past the ceiling?*

Maybe you're a worshiper. You love attending services and singing out to God at the top of your lungs. You don't even need to be in a church setting because sometimes you and God alone on a long drive is enough. You turn on your favorite worship playlist and pour out your heart to God. However, as soon as the service is over or as soon as someone cuts you off on the road, the euphoria quickly dissipates. It's easy to wonder, *Did I not do it right? Why can't I live in constant communion with God?*

Maybe you're action oriented. You prefer to be serving, giving, working, and helping. You love the mission trips your church goes on. You thrive in the local soup kitchen. You can work for hours helping others. But you can't escape the thought, *Is this enough?* You really don't know the Bible as well as your friends. You aren't sure if you pray enough. Secretly you wonder, Am I doing this "Christian thing" right?"

Whatever your efforts are to connect with God, you're not alone.

> You can work for hours helping others. But you can't escape the thought, *Is this enough?* . . . Whatever your efforts are to connect with God, you're not alone.

History is filled with people who sought God's attention and wanted his smile upon them. For review, let's start in the Bible.

The first had to be Cain and Abel—the sons of Adam and Eve. The boys grew up outside of Eden and had never known what it was like to have walked with God in the cool of the day like their parents had. So getting God's attention and gaining his favor was something that was not only new to them, but something they sought to attain. They each prepared offerings to present to God, but someone went cheap. While Abel brought a gift that was both extravagant and intentional, Cain brought leftovers. Abel brought meat, and Cain brought grain (is this proof God is not a vegetarian?). Whatever the case, Abel's sacrifice was accepted and Cain's was not. Their story tells us very early on that there are right and wrong ways to try and connect with God.

The Tower of Babel may be the next one. Was it pride or passion that caused these foolhardy people to decide to build a tower toward heaven? They wanted to make a name for themselves. They wanted to touch the sky. They wanted to be godlike in their presence and notoriety. Was this an attempt at immortality? At any rate, it seems to be a rather pronounced effort to be noticed by man, disguised as a method to reach God.

Fast-forward to the New Testament and you see the Pharisees taking things up a notch. They received the Old Testament law and made it their priority to be close to God. They kept the laws and then some. They even had laws to keep the laws to keep the laws. These guys were the masters of overkill. No one would utter the name of God (Yahweh), so they shortened it to "Ya" (thus, Hallelu–Ya, or Hallelujah). When writing that name, they would write a letter and go wash themselves, then write another letter, and repeat. I'm sure they were grateful God's name was not Rumpelstiltskin. The problem with their way of life is that they were so focused on the law of God they couldn't see the Son of God when he arrived.

Simon Bar-Jesus was another person who tried to get God's attention. This guy was a magician who ran a pretty good game of parlor tricks until Peter came along with his miracles. Once Simon saw his crowd running to be healed by Peter, he begged Peter for these abilities. He even offered to pay for them. Peter was outraged at this man using God's power for personal profit, and so are we. But before I point a finger, I know there are times I've stooped to this. Maybe not for profit, but I know there are times I've sought a connection with God just to either impress him or impress others—to get what another person has or to amaze those who lack it.

This strange collection of efforts doesn't end there.

In AD 400 a man named Saint Simeon was also rather extreme. He joined a monastery at the age of sixteen, but even this proved to be too worldly, so he shut himself in a hut for three years and went the entire time of Lent without eating or drinking. After this, he moved to the desert to "imprison" himself in a small cave, but too many people would seek him out, asking for him to pray for them. So Saint Simeon finally decided to withdraw as much as he could. He had a pillar erected fifty feet in the air, where he built a small platform to live out his days up there in communion with God until his death. He stayed on the pillar for thirty-six years.[1] (And you thought the Sunday service was long.)

Catherine of Siena lived in the 1300s, and she would practice self-punishment to connect with God. Some of her odd practices included drinking from sores, drastic fasting, and even inserting sticks down her throat to make herself vomit after eating. She became known as Saint Catherine.[2]

This practice of self-punishment was derived from some of the apostle Paul's teaching of "buffeting" his body till he became more holy.[3] Years later this was taken very literally in an expression of "corporal mortification." One would actually punish one's own body as a spiritual discipline. As strange as this sounds, it was used by such revered Catholic saints as Francis of Assisi and Thomas Moore.

Creative and painful ways to connect with God are not found only in the past, but also in the present. Recently the news has chronicled the adventures of Carl James Joseph. Carl is referred to as a Catholic pilgrim from Detroit, Michigan, and has been living without money and depending on the generosity of others for twenty years. He dresses like Jesus and even sometimes carries a cross down the street. Because of this, he has been given the nickname "The Jesus Guy." The Jesus Guy has now visited over twenty countries and has become a well-known figure in the old city of Jerusalem. When asked about all this, Carl states he simply wants to emulate his Lord.[4]

How Do *You* Try to Get God's Attention?

So is that what it takes to follow Jesus? Self-inflicted pain? Walking the streets in a robe while carrying a cross? Standing on a pillar for thirty years? Of course we'd say no, but don't we have our own version of this?

Some of us are pretty quick to punish ourselves for whatever wrong we've done or the lack of good we've accomplished. It's one thing to be convicted: "I need to say I'm sorry" or "I should have helped that man on the street corner." But it's another thing to feel condemned: "I don't deserve anything good" or "How could God ever use a misfit like me?"

Personally I've struggled with this. Sometimes after giving a message at a weekend service, someone will say, "Great message!" To which I feel obligated to say, "Oh, it was all God." I think deep down I believe if I don't deflect all praise, then God will stop using me. But is that true humility?

Or have you ever done this: You hear about a friend who is going through hard times and you think, *I should help them.* So you follow that conviction to take them a meal or give them some money anonymously. It feels good for a moment, but then you begin to think, *I should have done more. I could have given them my car, or house, or a kidney.* Obviously I'm being facetious, but many of us let conviction turn to condemnation: "I didn't do enough. God will not bless me anymore." And the self-mortification continues. Does this really help us connect with God? Does this really help us follow Jesus? Is this exactly what Jesus intended when he said, "Deny yourself, take up your cross and follow me"?[5]

And while we scoff at the Pharisees for their long lists of ways to keep God happy, don't we do the same? We may not have over six hundred laws to help us keep the law, but we look for biblical qualities to turn into lists: love God, love people, follow the Ten Commandments, abide by the fruit of the Spirit, learn from the Beatitudes, pray without ceasing, cast all your fears on Christ, take every thought captive, watch out for the weaker brother, heed the long list that starts 2 Peter, and of course listen to everything John tells the seven churches in Revelation.

These are certainly inspired, authentic words from God for how to live, but they move from life-giving to a death sentence when we see them as a to-do list for the favor of God.

One of the clearest ways I've seen this is with Bible reading. We all know we should read our Bible, and every day is best. I've tried devotionals in the past, but that seemed too easy. So I started memorizing of one verse at a time, but that seemed too little to read. Recently I did the "Read the Bible through in a Year" plan. That seemed noble enough, but many days I found myself just logging pages to get it done. So the guilt I removed from not reading enough was replaced with the guilt of not absorbing enough.

And that's just the Bible reading. Ever tried praying "enough"? I've kept lists and journals and taken prayer retreats and refrained from TV and spent hours listening to God all to be left with a feeling of "That's good, but it could have been more." Why do I do this? Think about all the prayers we learn, the psalms we recite, the Rosary beads, the Serenity Prayer, even the prayer of Jabez. These are all good. They are all centering. But they can often feel like they are not enough.

Even generosity can feel as though it is not enough. How much is "enough" to be considered generous? The Bible gives a number at 10 percent, a tithe, but is it enough to treat God like you do the IRS? "I'll give you what I owe you, but not a penny more!" It's possible to tithe, give to other charitable organizations, serve on mission trips, and still wonder, *Have I done enough?*

> Generosity can feel as though it is not enough. How much is "enough" to be considered generous?

Why do we often operate with this internal voice that says, "Good, but not great. Jump higher"?

Why do we do this to ourselves? What is it about these methods of self-mortification and self-imposed legalism that is so appealing?

Consider two reasons.

1. Control

There is something about knowing our list of things to do right that we enjoy because it allows us a sense of control over how God feels about us. After all, if I do all these things, then God is obligated to love me, bless me, and maybe even like me.

Recently, a family in our church had a child diagnosed with a rare form of cancer. We were all saddened to hear this news and we raced to their side. They were in shock and were still trying to get all the details for possible treatments and how to proceed. I recognize that in these situations our deepest fears emerge and our faith is shaken. Inevitably they asked the questions that we all ask at that moment: "Why did this happen?" "Why us?" "Why our child?" And then they followed it up with what many of us wrestle with: "We are good people. We love God. We do what he says. So . . . why?" I recognize that our worst theology comes out during the most difficult of times.

Why is this happening to me? After all, I've checked off all the boxes and done everything God said. We had a deal. I obey. He blesses.

I think this is what Jesus was cautioning us on when he said,

He causes his sun to rise on the evil and the good, and sends rain on the righteous and the unrighteous.[6]

God is not always fair. And he gives to whom he wants. And he seems to be using a different playbook than just who keeps all the rules.

The problem with our trying to itemize and categorize our relationship with God is that we can't control God or force his hand. And every now and then he reminds us. Which is so frustrating for those of us who like to know "how to succeed" at everything we do. Legalists and perfectionists like lists and rules so we can control our lives, our blessings, and sometimes our God. But even though God gives lists, he still cannot be controlled.

2. Score-keeping

There's another reason we are drawn to these types of discipleship methods. It's easier to keep score. We can determine how "good" we are and we can determine how "bad" someone else is. Furthermore, when we don't feel we are very good, we can just look at someone worse than us and not feel so bad anymore.

Isn't this what made the Pharisees so mad? They kept all the rules of what to eat and who to associate with, and when Jesus wouldn't eat with them they said, "He eats with sinners."

I know I went through years of being a closet Pharisee. I criticized those who smoked, drank, swore, had long hair, got tattoos, played the lottery, listened to secular music, and drove over the speed limit. It was easy to evaluate my success by what I *didn't* do, and it was easy to judge someone else's spiritual maturity by how many of these vices they avoided. But one day it hit me. I was moral. I was virtuous. But I didn't truly love anyone, and Jesus said a lot more about loving others than he did about cigar smoking or dancing. Jesus didn't seem to keep score. Jesus seemed to just love others.

Now, I know the pushback: "But we Christians are called to a different way to live. We are called to be renewed and transformed and to work out our salvation with fear and trembling." But it seems that there must be a way to do this that is less self-serving. How would Jesus really want us to follow him? What is God really expecting? And how do we protect ourselves from letting our efforts to connect with God turn into efforts to impress others?

Could it be that the way to follow Jesus was given to us before we were even introduced to Jesus?

A Better Way

Around four hundred years before Jesus, we were given a proclamation from a prophet who was trying to get God's people to follow God again. They were God's royal priesthood, a holy nation, blessed to be a blessing, but they were living below their calling. They were consumed with hedonism, selfishness, and idol worship. They drifted into pits of despair, were obsessed with self-preservation, and wallowed in their own fears and misfortune. It is into this setting that the prophet Micah was called to bring a word of realignment.

I wonder if you need to hear those words. Perhaps you are stuck in what seems to be an endless cycle of selfishness, despair, self-preservation, and exhaustion. Perhaps you know what it's like to be stuck in the performance trap of religious perfectionism. Maybe you are wondering if there is another list you've missed or another scorecard to fill out. What does it really take to get God's attention, to stay in God's good graces, and to live a life in the center of his will and blessing?

The prophet Micah gives Israel words that will be overlooked and passed over, but, fortunately, passed on. From Micah's proclamation we can learn what God does look at, how God does judge the heart, and what we should focus on. It's not another set of tasks to add to our already growing religious to-do list; rather, it's a statement that encapsulates the heart of God.

Following Jesus is not always easy, but it was never meant to be complicated.

And starting in the next chapter, I hope you'll begin to see how three words, in particular, can change everything.

Granted, as my friend Mike Breaux said, following Jesus is not always easy, but it was never meant to be complicated.

TO-DO LIST

Create your own prescription label of the version of Christianity you are most familiar with along with its own "fine print." Take note of what you include in both, as this can help you view the rest of the book from your own beliefs and/or experiences, as well as give you something to build on or goals to set in order to deepen your relationship with Jesus.

DISCUSSION QUESTIONS

1. What's the most interesting thing you've ever done, or heard of someone doing, to try to get God's attention?
2. Why do you think we make following Jesus so complicated?
3. Based on what you've read, know, or have experienced about Jesus, what do you think he expects of us in our own time and place?

two

What Micah Learned in Sunday School

Growing up in the Midwest and growing up in church meant one thing: Every Sunday I'd not only be in church, but also in Sunday school. Sunday school was an hour of instruction that dates back as far as the 1700s, but really began to flourish as a ministry for children and even adults in the 1950s. It became a great tool of outreach to gather kids from all over and teach them the Bible. Some churches even had "bus ministries" to get kids there. Kids would gather in classrooms where volunteer teachers would instruct them in Bible stories.

So on Sunday mornings I would put on my all-white suit, grab my twenty-pound Bible, and get in the car with my parents and sister. Sunday school was at nine, followed by church at ten. If the pastor didn't talk too long, we'd be home before the roast over-cooked in the Crock-Pot and the NFL games kicked off.

Sunday school at my church served many purposes.

For adults, it was a place to catch up with friends, drink cof-fee, and eat donuts, and someone would teach a lesson while the participants would play out their personality types: The introverts would take notes, and the extroverts would make entertaining banter or insightful comments with the teacher or rest of the class. Crowd participation was one of the big differences between a Sunday school class and a church service.

For some adults, kids' Sunday school provided free childcare. After they dropped their kids off for Sunday school, they'd head to the Pancake House till church began. I guess they preferred a short stack to a glazed donut.

But for kids, this was a great way to have an interactive experience at church. Sunday school in the 1970s was where we had great technology like flannel boards. These boards, literally made out of cardboard covered in flannel, would serve as the backdrop for paper cutouts of biblical characters. Funny how Mary and Moses often looked the same. Budget restraints, I guess.

Snacks were often included. While adults got donuts, kids got saltine crackers. Sometimes there were songs and crafts, but there would always be a lesson.

Sitting in Sunday school I heard many of the classic stories. I remember learning about Noah and the ark. Such a sweet story depicted with happy animals marching two by two onto the big boat. Noah was smiling, the animals were happy, and this was a lovely depiction of God's provision during a difficult storm. What was never discussed were the screams of drowning people floating in the waters. We got the G-rated version. Not even PG, let alone PG-13.

Not only did we learn about Noah, Moses, Abraham, Mary and Joseph, Jesus, and the apostle Paul, we also heard about fun animals like donkeys that talked and whales that were kind enough to spit prophets back on dry land. That was my experience at Sunday school in the 1970s. And the stories I learned stay with me even to today.

More Than Just Stories

Micah had a similar experience.

Granted, it wasn't on Sunday, since Micah was Jewish. But he still had his version of Sunday school. Before Micah was a prophet who penned one of our books of the Bible, he was a kid going to church, or temple, with his parents. I wonder if he had a white suit, or robe, and if he watched the clock hoping the roast wouldn't burn.

Micah grew up in the southern kingdom of Judah in a little town near Lachish called Moresheth. Not so much the suburbs, but more of the farmland. Micah was a prophet of the blue-collar folks who tended the fields more so than those in the town square in urban Jerusalem, around the Temple, which would have been more Isaiah's scene, another would-be prophet around the same age as Micah. In fact, the two may have even crossed paths. I like to think that while they probably didn't go to Sunday school together, they might have met at summer camp. No doubt they grew up on the same stories.

While we call them Bible stories or even stories from the Old Testament, these stories were so much more than that for Micah. They were the history of his people and their relationship with their God. These stories formed their identity.

Micah would have seen the story of creation as more than a technical timeline of the beginning of the world. He would have viewed it as more than a scientific method that needed to be weighed against evolutionists and Big Bang theories. He would have seen it as how Israel's God, the one true God, spoke life into nothing. Brought light out of darkness. And how the Creator desired a relationship with his creation. He would have known his God as more than provable, but as a God who was powerful and yet somehow intimate. In a world filled with mythology and stories of gods and creation, this story proved different for

Micah. His God created humanity for a relationship . . . not simply as slaves.

The story of Noah was more than a fun flannelgraph with animals and a boat. It was the story of how his God was both just *and* merciful. Unlike the temperament of other so-called gods, the God of Israel didn't destroy everyone. Micah's God has a soft spot for people.

The story of Abraham was more than a classic tale of how you can be used by God at a late age. It is the story of God defying all odds and bringing life out of what seems to be death. The elderly couple, Abraham and Sarah, will have a baby, perhaps the first birth covered by Medicare. Micah's God . . . is a God who is still creating.

And it is to Abraham that God gives Micah's people their marching orders. They are blessed by this God. Not just to consume, not just to be spoiled, not just to win battles and conquer cities. They are blessed . . . to be a blessing.

> The Lord had said to Abram, "Leave your native country, your relatives, and your father's family, and go to the land that I will show you. I will make you into a great nation. I will bless you and make you famous, and you will be a blessing to others. I will bless those who bless you and curse those who treat you with contempt. All the families on earth will be blessed through you."
>
> Genesis 12:1–3 NLT

These stories that Micah grew up with were the values and covenants and mission statement of his people. They were created and blessed by the one true living God in order to be a conduit of that blessing to the rest of the world.

And Micah surely would have heard the stories of the Judges. The rulers God used as a conduit between himself and his people certainly oversaw the best of times and the worst of times. Speaking of these stories, where were these when I was in Sunday school? I don't recall a flannelgraph depicting Ehud plunging a sword into a king who was so fat the sword was swallowed up. And what about during the time of Deborah when Jael killed a neighboring king by driving a tent peg through his head? I think I would have remembered that! But whether or not Micah had a flannelgraph, he would have known the stories. For these stories were of great victory, then of great defeat. Micah would have heard what happened when Israel stopped following its primary mission—and that would be pain.

For generations we see this pattern over and over again.

Sin/Servitude/Surrender

The people disobey God for years. So God allows a neighboring nation to storm in and force them into slavery for years, until they finally cry out to God in humble surrender. This pattern goes on for generations. They churn through twelve judges over three hundred years spinning through this sin cycle. They sin, they are enslaved, then they surrender. This is literally a living out of the phrase "Those who don't learn from history are destined to repeat it."

This pattern continued with their kings. Saul was bad, then David was good, then Solomon started good and ended bad. Then the kingdom split and you had a whole host of bad kings with a few good sprinkled in. Israel becomes the northern kingdom and Judah becomes the southern kingdom with Jerusalem as its capital.

Micah is growing up under the rule of King Ahaz, a king who had devoted himself to pagan worship, building shrines, and seeking the help of any religion he could find. He even sacrificed his own sons, burning them alive in a ritual to the idol Molech. Not really a king worth following. Micah also lived during the time of Hezekiah, who was a pretty intense ruler himself. Hezekiah initiated several different religious reforms in the southern kingdom of Judah. He tried extremely hard to protect Judah against the threat of the Assyrian empire, including teaming up with some neighboring nations that they didn't really get along with in the past against Assyria's king.

Under Hezekiah, Judah experienced an economic boom. Wealth was invested into the land and led to growth of the larger businesses, but it collapsed many of the smaller ones. In other words, the wealthy landowners in the suburbs were profiting and getting wealthier off of the smaller farmers farther out in the country. To make matters worse, many priests and so-called prophets viewed their own ministry as a business rather than a calling by God. So Micah was speaking out during a time of radical change and anxiety. God's people were losing their identity, forgetting their story, and were threatened with losing it entirely if taken over.

Yet despite the fact that Micah and Micah's parents and their contemporaries had grown up with these stories of what happens when you disobey God, the people of Israel and Judah were slow learners. It wasn't just the kings who did evil in the eyes of the Lord, the people did as well.

The Other Gods We Worship

Micah grew up in a society that was also rather inquisitive of other gods. Still today we have an innate need to define where we came from, who provides sun and rain, who makes crops grow, who ensures our reproduction and ability to sustain life. It's just hard-wired in us—we have a need for God. But in an attempt to understand their own existence, the Israelites were drawn to Babylonian gods like Marduk and the Assyrian god Ashur. And in an attempt to get all the luck possible in having children, they would even pray to the Canaanite goddess Asherah and to Baal.

Not only that, the Israelites would become interested in the same god we serve, the god of *me*. After all, they were the only nation that had rules from their God—Ten Commandments for their covenantal relationship with him. So from time to time they would peek their nose over the fences of neighboring countries and say, "Why do they get to do whatever they want? Sure, they have their gods they worship and present sacrifices, but they can worship whomever they want. They can sleep with whomever they want. They can steal what they want and kill anyone who gets in their way. They are their OWN god. They are their own boss. They call the shots. Why can't we?"

Sound familiar?

Despite all the lessons we've learned from history, don't we often repeat the same mistakes over and over again, hoping for a better result? Lysa TerKeurst in her book *What Happens When Women Walk in Faith* says, "We are amazingly similar to the Children of Israel. We spend half of our lives looking back at our own Egypt with selective memories, longing to have our comfort zone back. Then we spend the other half wishing our days away for a dreamy future in our own promised land."[1] We look at our neighbors sleeping in on Sunday morning and think, *Must be nice.* We look at our friends having wild parties and spending their money however they want and think, *That's real freedom.* Don't we watch TV shows and see promiscuity and revenge and think, *That looks so satisfying?* We peek over our neighbors' fences or stalk their social media pages and think, *I'd like to do that too. I'd like to have no accountability, no religious norms, and do what I want, when I want, with whom I want.* We are just like a five-year-old. And we are just like the nation of Israel.

> Despite all the lessons we've learned from history, don't we often repeat the same mistakes over and over again, hoping for a better result?

This is not the only way our story is like the people of Israel and Judah in Micah's day. Another growing concern for Micah was how his people were abandoning their call to be a blessing to others. They had settled on pursuing the allure of "more." More comfort, more stuff, more riches. As a result, the wealthy class was on the rise at the expense of the poor. This is not a surprising result if we take God's rightful place in our own lives. When we call the shots, we are drunk with power and greed. God is the only one equipped to truly handle glory and riches. He uses them for the provision of his children. We use them for the pleasure of ourselves.

That's how Micah's story intersects ours. He's living in a 700 BC version of our world. Because people are people. And we're all broken.

Micah has to be shocked. He's heard the stories of how God is Creator . . . then why do they worship Ashur? If God is the one who brought fertility to Abraham and Sarah in their nineties, why would anyone worship Asherah? If God is the one who has given us the mission to bless others, why would we live for ourselves?

So here's the state of Micah's world: far from God. Looking over the fence at other kingdoms with no rules, and being envious. Living with no boundaries. Eating from the tree. Living like the people of Noah's day. No longer a blessing or blessed, and destined to be like the times of the judges.

> Someone has to decide, This is enough! Wake up!

In all tragic stories of injustice and unfaithfulness, there comes a point where someone stands up and says, "Enough is enough." Movies like *Norma Rae* and *Erin Brockovich* show us modern-day stories. We know of great movements led by Nelson Mandela and Martin Luther King Jr. Someone has to decide, This is enough! Wake up!

This is what motivates moms and dads to join the PTA. This is what motivates lawyers to do pro bono work. This is what motivates college students to start nonprofits. This is what motivates empty-nesters to decide to foster kids. It's God-breathed. And it's what God uses to get his message out and his mission advanced.

When the children of Israel were lost and astray, God used prophets. And in this case, God used Micah—motivated by the stories from Sunday school, brokenhearted by the reality of his culture. God arms Micah's holy discontent with several visions of what is about to happen if Israel continues on this path. And it is Micah's job to pass these along to his people. This is the NEW Sunday school curriculum.

Micah's Message

So God uses this holy discontent in Micah to share some visions—visions of what will happen if they won't return. Micah writes these down and proclaims to his people words of God's impending judgment.

> Hear, you peoples, all of you, listen, earth and all who live in it, that the Sovereign Lord may bear witness against you, the Lord from his holy temple.
>
> Micah 1:2

These visions will contain images of exile and suffering. The days of peace are coming to an end. Assyria threatens.

Not long after this, as the people are seeing this prophecy come to bear, the prophet Jeremiah will reference what Micah says:

> Micah of Moresheth prophesied in the days of Hezekiah king of Judah. He told all the people of Judah, "This is what the Lord Almighty says: 'Zion will be plowed like a field, Jerusalem will become a heap of rubble, the temple hill a mound overgrown with thickets.'"
>
> Jeremiah 26:18

The end is near.

And Micah warned them.

Now, what does all this have to do with you and me trying to follow Jesus? Many of us are just hoping to have prayers that make it past the ceiling. We are just wanting to understand the Bible enough that we can answer our kids' questions they always seem to ask at bedtime. We are just wanting some indication that we are doing enough to get a smile from God rather than a look of disappointment. Even though we may not have heard Micah's story in Sunday school, we wonder what good it does us to hear it now.

The hidden gem in Micah's prophecy is that he tells the wayward people how to return to God. He gives them the process it would take to have prayers answered, questions make sense, and God's favor to rest upon them once again. This ancient document was saved, preserved, and revered years later, but was ignored in its day. And this ancient document not only clearly states how to return to God, it sets up the road map for how to follow his Son, who will arrive seven hundred years later.

Micah starts off with describing our predicament: How will we get right with God?

> With what shall I come before the Lord and bow down before the exalted God? Shall I come before him with burnt offerings, with calves a year old? Will the Lord be pleased with thousands of rams, with ten thousand rivers of olive oil? Shall I offer my firstborn for my transgression, the fruit of my body for the sin of my soul?
>
> Micah 6:6–7

Here, the word *exalted* simply means "heights." And Micah is asking, "How do we come before this God who is so high above us?" Isn't that how we feel in our daily lives? We are so thick in the routine of to-do lists, carpool schedules, soccer tournaments, project reviews, dentist appointments, and homework that we think, *God is so high above this. He's on another level. He sees all and deals with all. He's dealing with the cosmos, the climate, the continents, and the Kardashians. How does he even see my busy little life? How would I even get his attention? How would I just get in good with him, let alone have a relationship with him?* So our natural reaction is theirs—try making a big, gaudy sacrifice.

In Micah's time that might be burnt offerings, young calves, herds of rams, or maybe rivers of oil. Then there's the Canaanite practice of sacrificing your firstborn. For us, a "sacrifice" might be going to church six weeks in a row. Taking notes. Maybe it's finally giving some money in the offering plate. Perhaps it's doing a Beth Moore Bible study or deciding to keep a prayer journal. Maybe it's trying to stop swearing, or drinking less, or staying off certain websites. "Oh, I know, what if for the next thirty days every post I make on social media is a Bible verse?" Certainly these things will get God's attention. Certainly these might make God grant me my request, or at least lay off the punishment I feel I may have coming.

That's the way the Israelites thought. Yet Micah says it's so much simpler. He sums it up this way:

> He has shown you, O mortal, what is good. And what does the Lord require of you? To act justly and to love mercy and to walk humbly with your God.
>
> Micah 6:8

Justice. Mercy. Humility. That's it.
Seriously? What's the catch? Where's the fine print?
Everything God has told us to do can be summed up in this statement. Everything God was asking the nation of Israel to be can be summed up in three words. The family of Abraham, the

call to be a blessing, the Ten Commandments, the creeds of the Judges, the cries of the prophets, and eventually the call to follow Jesus all come down to act justly, love mercy, and walk humbly with our God.

Justice. Mercy. Humility.

Being a part of the kingdom of God is to be part of the mission of God. And that mission is to bring heaven to earth.

How do we do that? First, we need our sin forgiven. Jesus does that. Paul tells us in Romans 6:23 that though the wages of our sin is death, the gift of God is eternal life in Christ Jesus our Lord.

> Being a part of the kingdom of God is to be part of the mission of God. And that mission is to bring heaven to earth.

The statements Micah makes do not comprise the way of salvation, but rather the way of sanctification—what we do after we are saved. In other words, now that we are part of the family of God, here's how the family behaves.

We need to be in right standing with God, and Jesus does that. Now what? Well, we are blessed not just to be blessed, but to be a blessing. How do we do that? How do we seek and save the lost? How do we bring heaven to earth? How do we live out the Ten Commandments? How do we see the fruit of the Spirit in our lives? How do we love God and love people?

Act justly. Love mercy. Walk humbly . . . with our God.

This is exactly what Jesus will do. He shows up ushering in this new kingdom. He shows us what it means to be blessed to be a blessing. He empowers us with the Holy Spirit. Religion is gone, and a relationship with God remains. All that is left is for us to join in.

How? The same way.

We're going to dig in to these three words. But first, let's talk about how they are lived out: with our God.

TO-DO LIST

Reflect on some practices, habits, events, or beliefs of your own that were influential at one point in your life but have since become less so. Write down what changed for you, how you adapted to that change, and perhaps what you hope to change in the future.

DISCUSSION QUESTIONS

1. Who are some figures (they can be from the Bible or not) who have personally inspired you to follow Jesus better or become a better person?

2. Can you relate to the cycle of sin/servitude/surrender in your own life? Where do you long to break that cycle the most? In yourself? Your community? The world?

3. Why do you think something so simple and obvious as "do justice, love mercy, and walk humbly with God" is so rarely practiced or taught?

Step 1

↓

WITH GOD.

three

Your God May Not Be THE God

Saturday with my wife is not complete without her dragging me to Hobby Lobby. I obviously don't have to go, but if I want to spend time with her, then Saturdays are made for a trip to Hobby Lobby. I see it as quality time. She sees it as bringing someone to carry things.

For those who do crafts and home decor, Hobby Lobby is a panacea of options. You can create floral arrangements, change out hardware on old furniture, and even find enough scrapbooking supplies to chronicle the life of each Duggar child. But for most guys, well, it can feel like a maze you can't escape. No one gets out without spending two hours and two hundred dollars. On a good day.

So one day while killing time as Lorrie combed each aisle, I thought I'd investigate the wall hangings. There were plenty of folksy sayings like "Farmhouse Rules" or "I do my ironing in the dryer," but I was surprised by all of the Bible verses. I've read David Green's book about the beginnings of Hobby Lobby and its Christian roots, and I could even detect the instrumental worship music playing throughout the store. But as I glanced through all of the plaques, canvases, and wood carvings, there were a lot of Bible verses inscribed.

It was not a surprise to see John 3:16. That one has been a popular magnet, bumper sticker, wall art, and World Series sign ever since Gutenberg printed the Bible. It was not a surprise to see Psalm 23. We've relied on comfort from "The Lord is my shepherd" since *shepherd* was listed as a career choice in high school.

Over the past few decades, a couple new ones have risen on the popularity charts. Proverbs 3:5–6 ("Trust in the Lord with all your heart . . .") was risky because it was two verses instead of one—but hey, Psalm 23 was a whole chapter. And these two verses gave great clarity on how to trust in God. Then came the prayer of Jabez. This rather obscure collection of verses was seemingly discovered by Bruce Wilkinson in the early part of the twenty-first century.[1] Yes, it had been around since it was written by Ezra in the fifth century, but Bruce might have been the first to read it. Just kidding, of course.

These greatest hits of wall hangings made sense to me. What surprised me was seeing Micah 6:8: "Act justly, love mercy, and walk humbly with your God."

Maybe it was the reclaimed wood it was on or the instrumental version of "El Shaddai" playing that got me, but even though I had read this verse before, I was struck anew by its depth and its simplicity. And yet it can also be rather subjective, depending on how you define the last three words: "with your God." Knowing your God will determine your level of justice, your definition of mercy, and your degree of humility. So let me ask you . . .

What Determines Our Closeness with God?

Let me give you two scenarios.

The first is individual A, a fugitive of the law who has been arrested multiple times and spent years in jail. He never read his Bible, and he was not consistent with his church attendance due to his travel schedule.

The second is individual B. He was married with kids. He went to church every weekend. He served as a deacon. He led the Boy Scout troop and worked as a public servant.

Which one is the true follower of Jesus? (You know I'm setting you up, right?)

Individual A is the apostle Paul. He never read his Bible because he was still writing it. And he wasn't involved in a local church because he was traveling around starting them. Granted, he was in jail due to his preaching, but still, he was not regarded as a pillar of society or a great citizen.

Individual B is Dennis Rader. He was arrested in 2005 for multiple murders, as he was discovered to be the serial killer of Wichita, Kansas, known as the BTK killer. Appearances can be deceiving.

Each of these individuals had a definition of what it meant to act justly, love mercy, and walk humbly. The difference was who was behind that definition. For Dennis, it was himself and his twisted ethos. For Paul, it was Jesus.

Seem a bit extreme?

What about you and the person next door?

You go to church, they don't. You read your Bible, they don't. You give to those in need, they give to their local sports programs and museums. You think they are wasting their time and money. They think you are. It all comes down to who your God is.

Now, I know what you're thinking: My God is THE God. You know, the one true God. Big guy in the sky. The man upstairs.

Of course. But let me ask you some questions.

Questions to Know What God You Serve

1. Where does your mind drift?

When you are in the car stuck in traffic, or when you are sitting in a boring meeting, what do you daydream about? I'm not talking about the natural things—like what's for dinner or did I close the garage door? Nor am I talking about the weird things that pop up from the past, like suddenly I'm thinking about a touch football game I lost in fourth grade or an episode of *Knight Rider* I can't forget. I'm talking about the things we worry about, or fixate on, or are always trying to fix, solve, or revise from history. That stupid thing I said in a meeting and now everyone probably thinks I'm the dumbest person on staff. My mind drifts to regrets from the past, or possible success in the future, and if I could just do this one thing then everyone will be really impressed. What do we call something that consumes our attention and promises to change our lives? We call that a god.

2. What scares you?

What scares you more: There is no God, or there is no more money in the bank? There is no God or there is no more job? Even in my line of work—ministry—it can become easy to be more consumed about the work of God than a relationship with God. I fear losing my church, my congregation, my reputation . . . more than my connection with God. Maybe there's something in your life you think you can't live without. Your job. Your friends. God forbid, your spouse or kids. Your parents. Your reputation. What do we call something that we can't live without? We call that a god.

3. What do you pray about?

Now, this is a bit interesting, because we think that by praying we are good. After all, we are talking to God. But what is it you are saying when you pray? I notice that my prayers often drift to "God, help me . . . God, bless me . . . God, protect me. God, will you make everything okay for me? God, will you make my plans succeed? God, will you lead us not into discomfort and deliver us from pain?" I realize in this scenario that God is the servant and I am on the throne.

4. What does your calendar say?

Time is a good indicator of where your heart is. Make a quick list of your priorities. Most of us would say God, family, friends, work. But look at the last four to six weeks of your calendar. For most of us, the order is reversed. Obviously, we have to go to work, and that takes up a good chunk of our week, but what are we doing at work? Our best to serve our true master, God? Our best to serve others? And what are we doing when we are home? Cell phones down, focused on our kids and spouse, meeting their needs, serving them? Or are we trying to decompress from work and find some level of personal joy in hobbies, recreational activities, or stress relievers? And what about time with God? How many times are we in church, reading our Bible, praying, serving? What do we call something that dominates our time? A god.

5. What does your bank statement say?

It's common now to hear pastors say, "Show me your bank statement and I'll show you your heart." But it was Jesus who said it first: "Where your treasure is, there your heart will be." Now, I know you're thinking, *Well, I've got to eat and live indoors*, but let's take rent and food off the table. What do you spend your money on that brings you joy? How do you use your money to make you smile? Nothing wrong with golf memberships, home decorating hobbies, and even fashion compulsions, but does it hamper your ability to tithe and help alleviate others' suffering because of it? What do we call something that controls our finances at the expense of others? A god.

6. What do you look at on your phone?

There may be an app for everything. And while you and I may have dozens of apps on our phones, truth is we probably use only a few. And odds are they are social media apps. Most Americans look at their phones eighty times a day—once every twelve minutes—and what we are checking most often is Facebook, Instagram, and Snapchat.[2] And while we are looking at what others are doing, eating, and wearing, what we're really wondering is, *Did anyone comment on my post?* or *How many likes did I get?* What do we call something that demands our attention and determines our worth? A god.

Oh, we aren't Satanists. We're not worshiping the devil. We may not even listen to "Stairway to Heaven." But that doesn't mean we aren't worshiping the WRONG God.

> Our obsessions, concerns, anxieties, and time-wasters tell us more about who our god is rather than our proximity to church on Sunday morning.

Our obsessions, concerns, anxieties, and time-wasters tell us more about who our god is rather than our proximity to church on Sunday morning. As Beth Moore writes, "I don't think the biggest threat to our theology is humanism or the host of world religions. Our biggest threat is cut-and-paste Christianity. If man places his faith in a god he has created in his own image, has he placed his faith in God at all?"[3]

Think about our other gods. . . .

Our parents. We understand that many of our initial impressions of who God is come from the parental figures in our lives. They model discipline, love, nurturing, grace, justice, and mercy for us. They teach us how to live and what values to hold. For some of us this is a tremendous blessing. For others who grow up in dysfunctional homes or suffer at the hands of abusive parents or even feel the void of an absent parent, it can have a negative impact on our understanding of God.

I think about my upbringing. I had wonderful parents who loved each other and us kids, but they still had their imperfections. They suffered from what had been handed down to them, and they worked to not pass it along to us, but we are all human. So even though there were so many positive things about my parents that helped prepare me for an understanding of God, their flaws skewed my thoughts on God as well.

My dad had a favorite saying: "Son, if you do it right the first time, you won't have to do it again." This was said to me often in my growing-up years. Vacuuming out the car was not enough. There would be an inspection, then a verdict, and possibly a redo. I can recall painstakingly vacuuming over every inch of carpet on the floorboards, in between the seats, even the trunk. The only thing more disappointing than having to do it again was hearing the words from my dad, "You missed a spot." This gave me a skill set of discipline and follow-through for which I am daily grateful. But this also made understanding grace difficult. As I got older and heard biblical concepts of the grace of God, I thought, *Well, sure . . . if you get it right the first time . . .*

This view of God has been a set of glasses I struggle to take off. Actually, it's more like contacts that don't come out easily rather than glasses I can take on and off. I don't blame my dad, I just recognize how natural it is for all of us to view our god through the example of our parents. Which makes me question . . . If I'm serving, worshiping, and trying to impress a God who is always waiting to critique me or point out my faults, am I really serving the right God? What do we call someone who defines our worth, our view of grace, and our understanding of forgiveness? A god.

The parental issue can be expressed another way. I have a friend who is asking questions about faith. For much of his life he had what I call the "country music god"—a healthy respect for the man upstairs, but no relationship with God. No desire to submit to the lordship of Jesus. Just someone we tip the cowboy hat to during a prayer. Over several months, John and I developed a somewhat close relationship. I found out he lost his parents when they were relatively young and he had been living his life as a walking me-morial to them—occasionally praying to them, talking to them, making decisions to honor them. So after spending time at our church and asking questions about eternity, I asked him, "Are you sure of where you're going after you die?"

"Oh, I'm not sure, but I think I've been a good person."

I said, "Good people don't go to heaven. Forgiven people do. Are you ready to take Jesus up on his offer for forgiveness?"

He said, "Well, my parents never did, so I just want to go wher-ever they went." He is not alone.

For many adults who are progressing in faith, the mindset that holds them back is, *I don't want to go where my loved ones may not be. I don't want to dishonor my upbringing in another religion, even if I think Christianity is true.* What do you call someone who determines your eternity? A god.

Our country. Speaking of the country music god, another god that many of us struggle with is the god of country. For those of us who live in America, we love our country. We love its Christian heritage, its rich values, its generous spirit. We love our freedom for life, liberty, and the pursuit of happiness. We gladly defend it and sing about it and fight for it. But just because we are American does not make us Christians.

I grew up in Kansas. Most of my friends are Kansas Jayhawks fans. Many of them went to KU. They cheer like crazy for their basketball team. They try to ignore the football team. And every-where I go, people who find out I'm from Kansas assume I'm a Jayhawks fan. But I'm not. I'm a North Carolina Tar Heels fan. Why? It's a long story. But the reality is just because I'm from Kansas doesn't mean I'm a Jayhawks fan. I chose otherwise.

Following Jesus is a choice. And being raised in a country that has people who historically made that choice doesn't mean *you* have made it. What we tend to do is let our heritage, our parents' faith, and our feel-good values of God and country become our god. While others in the country have chosen to follow Jesus, if we have not yet chosen to do so, we aren't serving the right God. We are honoring someone else's god. Not ours.

> What we tend to do is let our heritage, our parents' faith, and our feel-good values of God and country become our god.

Our spiritual leaders. Let's get personal. I'm a pastor of a church. And I see how sometimes people see me as the "god" figure in their life. They hear me talk about God. They hopefully see me live like a Christ-follower. And when they have a prayer request they often ask me to pray for them. And I'm happy to do that. The danger comes when they see me as the only conduit they have to God. I've heard people say, "Will you pray . . . because God will listen to you." Why wouldn't he listen to *you*? Sometimes we put too much pressure on the church leaders in our lives. We assume they are godly, which leads to our viewing them like God. Then when they do something human, we resent them.

In the 1980s we were inundated with televangelists who raised money on TV for their ministries. While some of us were encouraged by their messages, many of us were repulsed. And what suffered? Our view of so-called godly people and thus our view of God.

This was even more devastating when the reports of abuse began to come out about some priests in the Catholic church. We were all horrified to hear these awful stories. And while priests were removed and settlements were paid out, the damage was done. The public no longer saw the church as worthy of trust . . . nor did they trust the God the priests serve.

What do you call someone who defines your view of deity, and your belief depends on their behavior? A god.

The home church I grew up in had its share of scandals. Several pastors were removed for various charges of misconduct. I remember seeing pastors come and go, but my parents never left. Why were they so faithful? Because they were committed to something bigger than a pastor. They were committed to God and to the people of this church. While their faith began due to a pastor, it was not fulfilled nor defined by the behavior of that pastor. My dad got that right the first time. And I'm grateful.

The Gods of the Israelites

The Israelites were off just a bit as well when it came to their view of God. While they wouldn't say that they had rejected Yahweh, the one true God, they would probably say they had just made some enhancements—like AFLAC, supplementary insurance. In other words, "We are so grateful for all that God has done to get us this far, but just in case he walks away, we've got some backup plans. Or worse, if he stays but just won't give us what we want, we need a Plan B."

The God of Fertility

We already discussed the Baal that the Israelites were drawn to. Why would they worship this stone idol? When you are unable to have children, you may be driven to any means necessary. You remember the lengths that Abraham and Sarah went to even after they had been promised by God they'd have a child? Sarah instructed Abraham to shack up with her servant to ensure a child in the family. As much as we want kids today, we'll go to many different lengths—in vitro fertilization, surrogacy, adoption. But in those days you didn't have those options. So the Israelites would bow down to any idol if it might help.

That being said, don't we often bow at the altar of family? Does your home's org chart look like this?

Kids
↓
Parents
↓
God

"What do the kids want to do? Where do they want to go? What activities do they want to do? We can't make church . . . soccer tournament. Kids can't go to church camp . . . volleyball camp." As parents, we give our kids a title they are not ready to hold: CEO. We turn into their personal chauffeurs and assistants, and then beg God to help make it all work.

The biblical model seems to be the opposite:

God
↓
Parents
↓
Kids

God is the head of the house. The parents submit to his mission, and the kids follow suit. It seems that most of our issues come when we forgo this model and worship family.

Think about what justice looks like when our family is our god. Justice always bends toward our family.

A few years ago we had some vandalism in our community. Some junior high students dumped some buckets of paint in a community pool. It caused hundreds of thousands of dollars of damage. The only recourse the authorities had was to ask people to turn in who did it. What do you think happened? Of course, no one said anything. We all want justice till we realize that the vandal is in our own home. Then we tend to turn a blind eye.

Think about how we define *love mercy* when our family is our god. Most of the mercy we extend is toward our own. We are merciful to our kids, we are merciful to their friends, we are merciful to anyone who might benefit our family. Certainly this is natural, but is it always right?

What about walking humbly? We humble ourselves to the will of our kids, to the will of our family, what they want, what they need. Isn't this biblical? Isn't the husband to lay down his life for his family? Isn't a mother to love her kids more than herself? Of course. But love and worship are two different things. To love is to sacrifice yourself for whatever is best for your kids. Even when they don't like it. Even when it isn't convenient for you. To worship is to yield to their will in all of our decisions. Not you? There's more to consider.

The God of the Sun

When you live in an agrarian society, your life can revolve around the weather. We need sun, we need rain. That's how we live. It's hard for most of us to conceptualize that today. Most of us rely on electricity more than the sun. Recently we had a power outage at home, and we quickly realized how much we needed our phones, TVs, and tablets. *Needed* may be an overstatement. But we may or may not have driven around in my car to charge up the phones and download a movie on a tablet. It was that type of dependence that the Israelites had toward the sun. And because of that, they'd do anything to keep in the sun's good graces.

Do you worship creation more than the Creator? Perhaps the creation we worship is the sun. We hike, we camp, we bike, we go to the beach, we go to the mountains, and we claim that we feel closer to God when we do. I'd agree. But to what expense?

When creation is our god, what does justice look like? Punish the poachers? Save the whales? Protect the environment? All things we should do. But do we have the same aggression toward sex traffickers, abusive husbands, and drug dealers?

Then when it comes to mercy, we tend to give mercy to those who create things we enjoy. It's easy to ignore big businesses abusing workers for a low wage as long as we still get their great service and tremendous products.

And what about walk humbly? If you are worshiping that which runs your business (e.g. money), don't you put it over God, over your family, sometimes even over your own health?

When my kids were very young, we were struggling to get the church going. It seemed like more late nights and meetings out with donors was the best way to go. But one Sunday, as I sat at a fancy restaurant dining on lobster bisque with prospective donors while my family sat at home and ate mac and cheese, I thought, *What am I doing?* I was humbling myself toward potential donors while making my family pay the price.

The God of War

The Israelites had a long history of successful battles. They'd known the spoils of victory from Jericho to Jerusalem. They'd conquered cities, burned down walls, and marched through with a mighty sword. But lately they'd had a bit of a losing streak. In Micah's time, they were being threatened by Assyria, and King Hezekiah wasn't budging. They were facing the prospect of being overrun and sacked. They'd been marched upon, and so on and so forth. Where was their victorious God now? What happened to their winning streak? Many began to think it was precisely because they weren't attacking back that they were being threatened. That God wanted them to go out and kill some more, and if they did, God would be with them just like he was with Joshua.

There were, however, others, such as Micah, who thought that time had passed and that they could still trust Yahweh over the power of empires and states.

> "In that day," declares the Lord, "I will destroy your horses from among you and demolish your chariots. . . . I will take vengeance in anger and wrath on the nations that have not obeyed me."
>
> Micah 5:10, 15

Remember, Micah was in a farming community. It takes a lot of resources to fund these types of wars that others in Israel were calling for. Perhaps he was calling for a more just and realistic way to deal with the Assyrians. Instead, perhaps he was calling his people to turn away from trusting the sword and "beat it in to plowshares" like Isaiah talked about. Or, as the psalmist wrote,

> Some trust in chariots and some in horses, but we trust in the name of the Lord our God.
>
> Psalm 20:7

We wouldn't say we have a "god of war" in our time, but we do like to win. Especially some of us type-A personalities; we would rather win an argument we don't even believe in than lose it. Some like winning so much they live vicariously through their kids and their successes on the soccer field, baseball diamond, or student body political realm.

If winning is our god, think how we define *act justly*. We are just when it serves our cause. Think how we *love mercy*. We are only merciful toward those who can pay us back or are not our competition. What about *walk humbly*? This is the humble stride we take to receive our trophy. And it all comes back to who is our god.

Before we can define these three terms, we must know what our standard is. We need to know who our God really is.

TO-DO LIST

Go through and answer the questions regarding "what God you serve" in the chapter, and commit to addressing those answers in real life by turning them over to God.

DISCUSSION QUESTIONS

1. Does the thought of a God who wants a deep relationship with us excite you or scare you? Why do you think this is?

2. What is the difference between honoring someone else's god and choosing to follow Jesus? (Think back to the example of the "country music god.")

3. Is a person's understanding or picture of God really that important? What difference does a person's view or understanding of God make in the way they live?

four

Who God Was to Micah, Jesus, and Now You

hat kind of name is Peb? I was thinking. Sitting in a boat in Montana one day, I was partnered with a fella named Peb—Peb Jackson, who I came to learn knew everyone. He was not a name dropper, but stories would come up. Friends with Eugene Peterson, buddies with Bono. I was a bit stupefied. Any names I could drop were meaningless in comparison to his contact list. We'd been together for about four hours, talking back and forth. I've never called anyone *Peb* that many times. Come to think of it, I don't think I've ever called anyone *Peb*. So finally I couldn't help myself. "Hey, Peb, if you don't mind my asking, where does your name come from?" This had obviously been a question he'd heard before, so he was armed with an answer. "My dad's name was Rock," he said, "and as I was growing up people said, "You're a chip off the block . . . or rock . . . so you're a pebble." And that got shortened to Peb. So, sixty years later I'm still Peb."

Names can be unique. Names can tell a story.

For instance, do you know where we get the name *jazz* for that style of music? It was originally called jas—short for the smell of jasmine perfume from the brothels in New Orleans, where the music originated. The name itself tells its history.

Names even change as we get to know people.

I'm not sure when we recognize our parents as our parents; it's almost as if kids just seem to always know: "This is my dad. This is my mom." That's what they told us to call them. It was nonnegotiable. They were the caregivers and the providers, and they seemed to have the food.

But do you recall when you realized they were people too? They had friends and feelings and plans that didn't involve you.

I was playing Little League baseball, and my dad was an assistant coach. I saw him as not just Dad, but Coach. *This guy is playing catch with me in the backyard. He's telling me how to stand and swing. He's giving me ideas on where to hit.* All the while I'm just trying to stay in the batter's box and not get hit. One game I'm sitting in the dugout, and Dad is coaching third base. Another dad is coaching first base. Suddenly, the first-base coach is yelling over at the runner on third base. What? Why? Then my dad, my coach, yells back, "Ed, you want to coach third too?" This man is Dad. And he is Coach. And he is Angry Coach.

You remember when you realized your parents had names other than Mom and Dad? I called my mom Mary one time and I thought her head was going to explode. "What's the big deal? Others call you that." She let me know that was not okay. All right. Point taken. So they are Bob and Mary to others, just not to me.

The mystery continues as you get to know your parents' high school friends or college roommates. It's no longer just Dad, this is "Wild Man" or "Hank the Tank." Suddenly these one-dimensional characters become 3D. Seeing them go through grief can be even tougher. Who are these people who are such a rock but now they are a puddle of tears at a funeral?

The older we get, the more complex people become, and the more complex we discover we are. If that's true for us, how much more is that true for God?

This is the God of the universe. The Creator of all. The designer of every personality, every number on the Enneagram, every species of animal, and every shade of the sky (not to mention 20,000 beetles). This God is complex. He is infinite. He is omnipotent. He is omnipresent. He is omniscient. How do you even begin to describe him?

Think about some of the more pedestrian ways we describe him. He's the Man Upstairs, the Big Guy, the One in charge, the Almighty. We have so many ways to try to explain the unexplainable.

When Micah says act justly, love mercy, and walk humbly with your God, what is he thinking of when he says "God"?

The Hebrews Had Many Ways to Describe God

Jehovah-M'Kaddesh means the God who sanctifies. Jehovah-Jireh means the God who provides. Jehovah-Shalom means the God of peace. Jehovah-Rophe means the God who heals. Jehovah-Nissi means the God our banner. El-Shaddai means "God Almighty." Adonai means Master or Lord.

Any of these names could influence how we understand this passage. Are we emphasizing the sanctification work of God? Or perhaps we are focusing on the provision of God? Maybe the almighty power of God? The name Micah uses means something. Not in terms of which God we are talking about, for there is only one true God, but in terms of the nature of God that is being emphasized.

What's surprising when you look at this verse in its entirety is, there are actually two names for God being used. And neither are the ones previously mentioned.

He has showed you, O mortal, what is good. And what does the *Lord* require of you? To act justly and to love mercy and to walk humbly with your *God*.

Micah 6:8 (emphasis added)

At first glance this is Hebrew parallelism. Like saying Dad and Father, two different words with the same meaning. But there is some significance to these.

The first word used for God (Lord) is *Yahweh* or *Jehovah*. Yahweh is associated with Israel, the name of the God of Jerusalem. This is almost the national name for God. This is a very personal name for God, which would have meant "To Be" or "I Am that I Am"—the name God uses for himself in the burning bush. He is contained. He is not leaving. He is seen only when you stand there for a while. It takes a while to notice that a burning bush is not being consumed. This nature of God is open enough to dwell within the temple, yet mysterious enough to hide away in the thick darkness as also indicated in the book of Exodus.

In Hebrew this would have been written with no vowels: YHWH. Sound it out: Yo-hay-va-hay. It sounds like breathing. Many Hebrew people believed this was God's way of signing his name on his creation—that with every breath we breathe, we breathe his name. In fact, even if we deny God's existence, we still utter his name with our every breath.

The second word used for God is *Elohim*. Elohim is connected with the cosmos, the nations. We see this name used in Genesis 1 as the name for God creating the heavens and the earth. The most intriguing part of this is that Elohim is plural, helping us understand the multifaceted personhood of God. It is descriptions of God like this that later influence Christians to develop the concept of God as Trinity.

While YHWH is personal and stationary, Elohim is big and vast and uncontainable. He stands outside of time and creation and hovers above the waters and walks among us. YHWH is the national deity of Judah, but Elohim is the God of the world and the cosmos.

So why does Micah use these both? Probably to provide the same emphasis that he does in the final verses of his letter where there is a focus on the question of who YHWH is. He is Elohim. He is above all, in all, through all.

Micah says in chapter 7,

"But as for me, I watch in hope for YHWH, I wait for Elohim my Savior: my Elohim will hear me." (v. 7)

"Who is a Elohim like you, who pardons sin and forgives the transgression of the remnant of his inheritance? You do not stay angry forever but delight to show mercy." (v. 18)

This God is one of justice and mercy. He is here. And he is everywhere.

Micah tells us to act justly, love mercy, and walk humbly not just WITH our God, but BECAUSE our God is that way first.

> **This God is one of justice and mercy. He is here. And he is everywhere.**

Our God Is Just

When I go to the amusement park and wait in line for over an hour with my kids, I want to ride the ride. So when someone cuts in front of me and no one says anything, I think, *Hey, you can't do that!* I start to process my options:

1. Politely ask them to go to the back of the line and wait like everyone else.
2. Notify a park official and report them.
3. Throw my $10 lemonade at his head.

Never once do I consider, *Oh, good for him. I hope he enjoys the ride.* Or, *I'm sure he's in a hurry so he needs to jump ahead.* Of course not! I want justice.

I've just stood in the heat and humidity for two hours. I've been forced to watch two teenagers in front of us hold each other like they are boarding the *Titanic.* I've been privy to the walking tattoo billboards behind us who apparently forgot to shower . . . this year. So forgive me if I'm a bit perturbed.

Whether we are at Disneyland, the DMV, or Walmart, we hate to be taken advantage of, whether in line or in the parking lot. We want things to be fair. We want justice.

Granted, those are all First World problems. What about the people who are caught in generational poverty? What about those oppressed by racism or sexism? What about the lack of education fueling illiteracy? What about those literally enslaved as cogs in the wheels of human trafficking? These are the people in need of justice, and yet they are often the ones without a voice.

There are organizations that stand up to speak out for those who can't. Our church has been working with an organization that is providing justice for those in need. They come in and rescue those who are oppressed, but they also set up laws to punish the oppressors.

In America there seems to be a cultural uprising to disprove or reject a traditional view of hell. Yet Canadian pastor Mark Clark talks of how most of the people pushing this are those who sit around Starbucks in suburbia and espouse their theories to make sense of a God they can't wrap their minds around.[1] But talk to anyone in a developing country who has felt the oppression of a dictatorship or the brutality of genocide: They are comforted by the thought that one day right will win and the evildoers will pay. They want justice.

This seems to make some of us uncomfortable. Probably because we have confused being just and being fair. *Just* is objective and based on predetermined laws. *Fair* is subjective and based on how you feel. For instance, when a police officer pulls me over and says I was going 65 in a 55 and he has to give me a ticket, he's being just. When I reply with, "But I wasn't going as fast as the red Corvette that was passing me," I'm asking him to be fair. "Since you let him go, let me go."

Our God seems to be just. All through the Old Testament, we see him establish the laws. If you eat from this tree, there is a price to pay. And Adam and Eve pay it. The plagues on Egypt seem a bit fierce—blood, frogs, the death of the firstborn. But God doesn't do it to be fair. He does it because he said he would. "I will bless those who bless you, and whoever curses you I will curse" (Genesis 12:3).

Jesus tells us a parable about our heavenly Father.

In Matthew 20 we read of a landowner hiring some day laborers in the morning for fifty dollars for a day's work. They agree and start working. About noon he goes out and hires some more. And then he hires some more around three o'clock. When quitting time comes, all the workers get fifty dollars, to which those who'd worked the whole day get a bit miffed.

> When they received it, they began to grumble against the landowner. "These who were hired last worked only one hour," they said, "and you have made them equal to us who have borne the burden of the work and the heat of the day." But he answered one of them, "I am not being unfair to you, friend. Didn't you agree to work for a denarius? Take your pay and go. I want to give the one who was hired last the same as I gave you."
>
> Matthew 20:11–14

It might not have been fair, but it was just. If our God leans toward justice rather than just being fair—as we consider fair to be—how should we emulate that?

Our God Is Merciful

We all like the idea of a merciful God. After all, that's what we all crave. The problem is we confuse mercy with being nice.

I recall one late night at summer camp when we were all in our bunks in the boys' dorm and mayhem began to break out. Kids started throwing things, yelling nicknames, laughing hysterically. Suddenly we heard the screaming of one young man, "STOP IT STOP IT STOP IT!" By this point, a camp counselor had had enough and turned on the lights. It was at this moment we all saw a boy up in the rafters dumping a bottle of shampoo on the kid yelling "STOP IT!" The lights are now on, all eyes on the criminal, and he is caught. Dead to rights. And he says, "It wasn't me." Really? You are still holding the dripping bottle of shampoo. He wanted mercy.

We all do.

We all stand before God with our own version of an empty shampoo bottle. The lies we told, the things we stole, the hearts we broke, the pain we caused. We've cost people years of happiness and tears of regret. We've grieved our family and our God. Jesus said to love one another, but we focused on loving ourselves. And when caught, when someone finally turns on the lights and exposes our deeds, we say the same thing: "It wasn't me." But we know it was. We just want mercy.

> We know what mercy is: not getting what we deserve.

It is in that moment that we know what mercy is: *not* getting what we deserve. Our sin means that we deserve punishment. We deserve to be separated from God and his goodness. And in that moment no one has to define mercy for us. We know what it is, because it's all that matters to us.

So let me ask you, in that moment, would you prefer God be merciful or just nice?

If I ask if you are a merciful person, you'd probably review how nice you are to people. I know I would. I said "Good morning" first to my neighbors. I let someone cut in front of me on the freeway. I gave a nice tip to the waiter. I smiled as I walked through the office and told people how great they are doing. I'm nice.

But when we are caught in our debt of sin, we need more than just nice. We need mercy. Mercy gives us what we don't deserve. Nice gives us pleasantries. Mercy makes us worship. Nice makes us reciprocate.

Our God is merciful. And thus he asks us to be like him—to LOVE mercy.

Our God Is Humble

We see God's humility in the world he created. In Genesis 1 we read that Elohim puts everything into motion for his glory, but also for his pleasure. God wasn't lonely; he didn't create us because he needed a friend. Rather, God wanted us to experience the community.

When the New Testament comes along, we see different persons of God at work. We see Jesus as God's Son, praying to God as his Father, through God the Holy Spirit, who is at work through God's people. This and the plurality expressed in the term *Elohim* came to be the benchmark for Christian theologians to develop the concept of the Trinity.

Though not an original Jewish idea, when you look back on some passages in the Old Testament, the Trinity does start to make a little more sense. When God—the Trinity—created humanity, the Jews now had an object for their affection, and it required their care. It required patience. It required love. It required mercy. And it even required saving.

What's beautiful about this is that God does not choose to use these qualities like we pick out a tool from the toolbox. God

IS these things, and asks us to become these as well. Our God is already and always has been a humble servant in equal submission to one another, and he now chooses to let us in on that. He stoops to serve us.

We see such a wonderful picture of this when Jesus himself stoops to wash the feet of his disciples. Look how John describes this:

> So he got up from the meal, took off his outer clothing, and wrapped a towel around his waist. After that, he poured water into a basin and began to wash his disciples' feet, drying them with the towel that was wrapped around him.
>
> John 13:4–5

Jesus humbling himself as a servant. But again, this is more than Jesus behaving like a humble servant. It's in his nature. Jesus *is* a humble servant.

Years later Paul is reflecting on the nature of Jesus, and he gives a very similar description to what we just read.

> Though he was God, he did not think of equality with God as something to cling to. Instead, he gave up his divine privileges; he took the humble position of a slave and was born as a human being. When he appeared in human form, he humbled himself in obedience to God and died a criminal's death on a cross.
>
> Philippians 2:6–8 NLT

Notice the parallels between these two texts:

- Jesus got up from the table / he gave up his divine privileges.
- He wrapped himself in a towel / he was born as a human being.
- He washed their feet as the servant / he humbled himself and died a criminal's death on a cross.

This IS God. He is a servant. He is humble. And he asks us to do the same.

When my wife and I were engaged and preparing to get married, we decided we needed to go pick out some furniture for our new place. So there we are, wandering around the furniture store, looking like a couple of wide-eyed wonders and thus an easy mark for any salesperson. It's at this time I notice the object of great affection for all men: a recliner. I'm thinking, *I'm about to be married. So I must have this. After all, this is where I will sit and watch TV and she will bring me food. And to top it all off, if you buy one, you get the other half off. Perfect.*

"Lorrie, this is perfect," I announce.

"Seriously? Buying two recliners feels like what we should do after we've been married fifty years, not about to get married."

Still, after some persuasion, I talked her into it. We didn't have much money, but we had just enough to pay for these chairs. We were promised the chairs would be handcrafted and shipped in about six weeks. No problem. But as life would have it, about a week later, we needed that money. Wedding prep is expensive. I lamented to my soon-to-be wife and her parents that I wished we hadn't purchased those chairs.

Lorrie's dad suggested, "Well, you could always go back and ask for your money back."

"Really?"

"Sure. Just take them your receipt and tell them you'd like your money back."

So that's what I did. I went in there, handed them the receipt, and asked for a refund. I received a quick "No," and could only respond with "Okay" as I left.

Later, when I mentioned it to my future father-in-law, he looked a bit puzzled. A few days later when I went over to visit my fiancée at her parents' house, my father-in-law handed me a check for the full amount of the chairs.

"How did you get this?"

"Well, I just went in and talked with them."

I was confused. "Did you make them an offer they couldn't refuse?"

He laughed. "No, I just questioned them long enough that they paid me to leave."

I was overwhelmed with gratitude, and had to ask, "Why would you do that?"

"Because I was once your age preparing to get married and needing every penny I had. I've been there before."

You know who our God is? One who's walked humbly, loved mercifully, and acted justly on our behalf. All because he's been there before.

TO-DO LIST

Pick a book of the Gospels and read through it while considering the question, "How does Jesus embody these characteristics that God demands in Micah 6:8?" Feel free to write down your observations or findings.

DISCUSSION QUESTIONS

1. How do the different names of God inform us about the different aspects of God's character?
2. What is the difference between justice and fairness? How are they similar?
3. What about mercy? How are justice and mercy different and similar?
4. What do the commands in Micah 6:8 tell us about God? About ourselves?

five

Leveraging the Full Power of God in Your Life

Standing in the ceiling-fan aisle at Home is daunting. There are so many options. What do I go with? Three blades? Four blades? Surely not more than five. I don't need to take flight. And what color? Every color from deep space black to hunter green to ivory coast is an option. And as overwhelming as that can be, the only thing worse is to bring it home. Now I've got a box I'm not sure what to do with.

Several things run through my mind. First, this is electric. We're not talking about hanging a picture and hoping for the best, we're talking about 110 volts. Touching the wrong wires while installing it could be a shocking experience. Or worse, I may not know I did it wrong, and one day while I'm out of town, an electrical fire might begin. This is serious business. Second, this is to hang over our bed. In an effort to not use the AC, this fan will be on and blowing while we sleep. The last thing I want is to have it fall on us in the middle of the night, knock us unconscious, and THEN cause an electrical fire. Suddenly I'm wondering if there's anyone who can help me put this thing in. But as most guys my age rationalize, *I'm a grown man. I can do this. This is my Everest.*

I begin opening the box and carefully pulling out each item. Four blades, one base, a bag of nuts, bolts, and wire caps. Done. I go outside and turn off the power. To the whole house. Can't be too careful. I then begin to dismantle the light fixture and set it aside. Easy enough. I take the ceiling fan base plate out and begin to fasten it against the ceiling. The instructions are impeccable. Apparently written by novices like me. Now the moment I feared. Attaching the wires. I begin to feel like I'm in *The Hurt Locker* and about to disarm a bomb. Red wire. Black wire. White wire. Even a green one. But thanks to the directions, I get it. I think this might actually not kill us. May even work.

At this point I'm getting excited. And when you get excited you start to rush. I pick up the pace as I finish mounting the motor. Then I begin to assemble the light fixture. Even put the bulbs in it. This is the easiest thing I've done yet. When it's time for the blades, I put one on and I'm so excited about what I've accomplished, I can't stand it any longer. I think, *I've got to see this thing work.* So I head out to the garage and throw the breaker back on. I smell for smoke on the way back into the bedroom, and it's all clear. Next step—turn on the switch. With excitement, I reach for the wall switch and flip it on. That's when the surprise comes.

The fan doesn't explode or even spark, but it is so out of balance that it spins around and it feels like the whole house is shaking. It causes such a ruckus that the bulb even shatters. Apparently these fans with multiple blades are supposed to have ALL the blades attached before you turn them on. I make a mental note. Then I spend the next week cleaning up glass.

Some things just don't work right until they are fully assembled.

There are many things that require all parts for them to work right.

Ever try to drive a car with only three wheels? Ever try to fly a paper airplane with only one wing? What about a refrigerator without doors? Full assembly required.

The same thing is true when it comes to our understanding of God. In the previous chapter we introduced how God exists in multiple persons: one God expressed in three persons also known as the Trinity. God the Father, God the Son, and God the Holy Spirit. If you've ever prayed for protection but feared punishment, you knew the Father but not the Son. If you ever prayed for direction but thought you were on your own, you knew the Son but not the Spirit. A fully functioning understanding of God requires a fully assembled God.

The Trinity is a baffling, mind-boggling concept. So much so that many Christians are almost ashamed to even mention it in passing conversation. How does that whole three-in-one thing work? We say we believe in one God, but why the three different distinctions? Why would anyone want to make this up?

The Trinity is an important concept because it is revealed by the character of God. The apostle John gives us some clarity:

> God is love. Whoever lives in love lives in God, and God in them.
>
> 1 John 4:16

We know what love is by looking toward God and examining God's character. How so? The Trinity expresses this because no one member of the Trinity can exist without the other. Each member of the Trinity gives itself over to the others and receives the others just the same. The Trinity is a constant giving and receiving of love; that is how we can describe this love of God. Love is God's nature because love is what God is and is constantly doing.

> Love is God's nature because love is what God is and is constantly doing.

But that's not where it ends. As you might suspect, there's a connection to Micah 6:8.

We need a fully assembled God to live a fully assembled Christian life as well.

As Fred Sanders writes in *The Deep Things of God*, "The Trinity makes all the difference in the world for practical things such as salvation, spirituality, prayer, Bible study, and church life. The doctrine of the Trinity is a practical doctrine, and has immediate implications for Christian life."[1]

It's Jesus' prayer that we actually live within this community known as the Trinity.

> "I pray also for those who will believe in me through their message, that all of them may be one, Father, just as you are in me and I am in you. May they also be in us so that the world may believe that you have sent me."
>
> John 17:20–21

Jesus says a couple of important things here. First, we at our fullest potential are to exist within the center of the Trinity. And second, when we do this, the world looks at us and believes in Jesus. What?

So that pressure we all feel to evangelize all of our friends, family, neighbors, and co-workers could actually be easier and possibly even grease the skids a bit when we do one thing—live *within* the Trinity?

Well, then, how do we do that? And what on earth does that have to do with justice, mercy, and humility?

I thought you'd never ask.

Micah 6:8 may not be describing the Trinity. That is a Christian doctrine that was added much later than even the time of Jesus. However, it certainly describes the character of God that the Trinity attempts to explain, and more to the point, how we can reflect that character in our own lives.

What is fascinating to me is that each of these persons of the Trinity are equal, each of them ARE God, and each have their distinct personalities. And each personality uniquely expresses one of these three qualities detailed by Micah.

The Just Father

Don't get me wrong, I'm not saying that the Son or the Spirit are any less "just" than the Father, but there is something that immediately makes us think about justice when we think about God the Father. Perhaps it's the stories we read about in the Old Testament. We envision the Father as being the one to evoke punishment on Adam and Eve. Lovingly, but strongly. They'd broken the rules. They must suffer the consequences. You can almost sense God weeping as he kills one of his creatures to yield its skin for covering for his rebellious children.

We envision the Father issuing the decree to Noah that he must send a flood to start all over. The sin and rebellion have gone on long enough. At some point he has to reach a breaking point, and now he has seen enough so he brings about justice. But notice the patience in the execution of this decree. Noah builds the ark for 120 years all while preaching to the scoffing crowd looking on. If any of them had repented and picked up a hammer, they would have been allowed on that boat. But none did. So it began to rain. And the Father cried great tears of justice.

But we also see the Father bringing justice down not just for the punishment of humanity, but the benefit of it. When we see Moses lead his people out of Egypt, there was justice against the Egyptians for the years of slavery and bondage of God's people, but then there was justice for the Israelites who were now free. And as they marched out of the dry Red Sea, they received freedom for a crime they had not committed. And when the Egyptians drowned in the collapsed Red Sea, they received justice for a crime they had committed.

This happens again in AD 33, outside the city of Jerusalem. Jesus, the Son of God, hung on a cross, receiving the judgment of a just God for the sins of all his children. And in that moment the Father gave justice to the sin for the benefit of the freedom of all of us.

> The Father gave justice to the sin, for the benefit of the freedom of all of us.

This is our God. This is our Father. He is just. He is not a dog without a bite. He is not a king without an edict. He will not be mocked. He will bring justice. It's in his nature. It is who he is.

Micah knew this side of God. He was living in the justice of the Father. The Israelites had tested his patience over and over and were now being threatened to experience the consequences of their rebellion.

So what does that mean for us?

If we are to live in the center of the Trinity, if we are to follow this God, we are to be people who revere the justice of God and administer the justice of God. So as we continue this discussion, ask yourself this one question: **Do I care about what the Father cares about?**

The Father brings justice *for* the weak, the poor, and the helpless. So do I care about those who others overlook? This is simple when we see a person on the street corner with a cardboard sign that says "Lost my job. Please help." That's an immediate obvious need. We give $5 and drive on feeling just and gracious. But what about the single mom at your office, whose income can barely make ends meet? Her ex-husband won't pay child support and no one is interested in helping her find legal aid. That one is hard to notice. What about the family at the end of the street whose daughter is enslaved by bullies at school because they have an inappropriate picture of her an ex-boyfriend took? They threaten to send it to their entire school if she doesn't do what they say. What about people on the other side of the world who sell their kids into slavery to make ends meet for the rest of their family, and then are never able to buy them back? The Father wants to bring justice to them. Do we care about what the Father cares about?

The Father brings justice *against* the arrogant, the proud, and the rebellious.

The Merciful Son

Even though the Father and the Spirit are merciful, we see the image of mercy lived out in the life of Jesus. Think about the day he was teaching to a packed house. The house was literally so full that no one else could get in to see him. But that didn't stop one group of guys. They hadn't come to stand outside and listen, they had come to see Jesus face-to-face. They weren't autograph seekers, they were miracle seekers, and they had a friend who needed the touch of God.

Their friend had been paralyzed since birth. Day after day he would wait for his friends to take him to the city courts to beg on the streets. But now there was hope. The miracle worker had come to town, and he was teaching in a house three doors down. These guys saw the people lined up around the block, but they made their way to the roof. They carefully hoisted their friend up with them and tiptoed over to the area where they assumed Jesus to be below. And then they began to dig. No shingles to worry about, this was a thatch roof. And no sense in being quiet. The noise would be overcome by the falling mud and straw. Finally, with no regard for anyone's home insurance, they opened up a big enough skylight to lower this man through the roof. There, before all these onlookers, he's dangled. Jesus takes one look at him and says, "Your sins are forgiven." That's nice, but that's not what they came for. And the crowd isn't buying it. So Jesus, knowing that everyone associated physical ailments with sin, proves his ability to forgive. He then says, "Stand up and walk." And the man does. Mercy on display for all to see.

Isn't this the same mercy we see when he says, "Let the children come to me" after the disciples have shooed them away? Isn't this the same gentle spirit displayed when Jesus touches a leper and heals him? A man who hasn't known human contact for years is not only healed but touched? Isn't this the same tenderness given to the thief on the cross? While Jesus is in excruciating agony, he has the kindness within him to extend mercy to a convicted yet contrite criminal. Everything about Jesus seems to be bathed in mercy.

So what does that mean for us?

It means mercy need not just be received but extended. We all want the mercy of God, we just don't want to show it. If we are to live in the center of the Trinity, if we are to follow this God, we are to be people who love, celebrate, and extend mercy. So ask yourself another question: **Do I see people the way the Son sees people?**

> If we are to follow this God, we are to be people who love, celebrate, and extend mercy.

When I see people who annoy me, Jesus sees people he died for. When I complain about slow service from my server at a restaurant, Jesus sees a single mom with two jobs trying to make ends meet. When I see neighbors who are up half the night hosting a loud party, Jesus sees people he misses. To be in the middle of the Trinity is to have the justice of the Father but the mercy of the Son.

And there is one more participant.

The Humble Spirit

Again, not to take anything away from the humility of the Father and the Son, but do you ever see the Spirit drawing attention to himself? We are not led to believe he has suppressed his power, but rather there's just no mention of it. This is the one whom Jesus referred to as "one that is better than me." Yet every time we hear about him, he's pointing to someone else.

In the beginning, we read he is hovering over the deep. He's simply giving praise to the work of God. Did he have a part of it? Of course. But he's highlighting the creation, not the Creator.

When he comes up on Samson and gives this fallen, blind warrior enough strength to literally bring the house down on the Philistines, he's not the one we are left talking about. It's Samson.

When he descends like a dove at the baptism of Jesus, no one is praising the Spirit or even mentioning the dove (if it was a physical dove). Rather, he is drawing attention to Jesus. "Look at him! The Father is well pleased!"

Even when he shows up like a rushing wind in the upper room of disciples after Jesus' ascension, no one can stop long enough to praise the Spirit for showing up and giving them powers untold. They all rush out to tell people about Jesus. And that is just what the Spirit wanted.

So what does that mean for us?

If we are to live in the center of the Trinity, if we are to follow this God, we are to be people who are comfortable with others getting attention that we may deserve. So ask yourself this question: **Am I comfortable with others getting the credit that I deserve?**

Do you cringe when someone else is being praised? Are you all right with someone getting heaped with compliments while you wait in the background? Are you able to quiet that voice in your head that is wanting to set the record straight, or telling you to "get what is mine"? Are you so comfortable being part of the work of the Trinity, or hidden within the Trinity, that you might not even be noticed? To be in the partnership with God is to have his mercy, his justice, and even his humility.

75

Just as you don't have the one true God without each of these distinct members of the Trinity, so, too, you don't have Micah 6:8 without each of its descriptions. You can't have justice without mercy, you can't have humility without justice, you can't have mercy without humility, and so on. If these things aren't life-giving and based on the love of God, they are not having the impact that they could potentially have, and they are not serving the purpose that they are meant to carry out.

Micah 6:8 is a calling for us to give our whole selves as offerings, not just the parts we're comfortable with or prefer. Furthermore, it is calling us to act in these three ways in a holistic manner. God and our actions based on who we believe God to be are inseparable. Those actions are inseparable from one another too.

This is the God we serve. And this is different from the God I thought I knew.

Years ago I had a bad first impression of someone. This person didn't say anything wrong, it was just the look on his face. I was talking with someone else and he was standing near, and his expression smacked of arrogance. And for some reason I never forgot it. From then on, anytime someone mentioned his name, I had negative thoughts about him. They could say something nice and I'd think, *Yeah, well, you must not really know him.* Occasionally over the next decade I'd see him again, and he would be fine. A couple of times we even had lunch and he was nothing but generous and gracious. But in the back of my mind I kept thinking about that first time I was around him.

Recently he called and invited me to lunch. I went begrudgingly and because I thought I was being the bigger man. But once again he was kind, complimentary, and even encouraging. Then something struck me as I drove away from that lunch. Could it be that I misread something long ago, and that wasn't who he really was? Maybe he was having a bad day. Perhaps he didn't even know how he appeared. Goodness, I get misread all the time. Was it fair to misjudge him for well over fifteen years? Perhaps my view of him was too small and misguided. I know I've done that with God.

What if the God we are to follow and serve and obey is more than a genie or a fairy godmother or cosmic judge? What if we saw him as a just Father, a merciful Son, and the humble Spirit who invites us into the center of their eternal friendship and can empower us to act the same?

TO-DO LIST

Consider how Micah 6:8 addresses the following questions by using the Trinity as a framework to do so.

- Who am I?
- Why am I here?
- How can I live successfully in God's eyes?
- How can I belong?
- What can I do about suffering in my life and the world?

DISCUSSION QUESTIONS

1. How does the concept of God as Trinity affect the way we live?
2. What aspect of the concept of the Trinity is most confusing to you or those you know?
3. What about this chapter was helpful in connecting God's character with our purpose within the world and how God sees us?

Step 2

↓

ACT JUSTLY.

six

The Two Sides of Justice

'm a sucker for superhero movies. And judging by the box office, I'm not alone. Though I'm a loyal Batman fan and truly believe him to be the greatest and most realistic hero of them all, I still enjoy all the rest—Iron Man, Black Panther, Captain America, Thor, The Flash, Wonder Woman, and all the Guardians of the Galaxy. Even though these superheroes have captivated the attention of many for the last couple of decades, Superman seems to be the one that has intrigued us the most if not the longest. The superlatives about him are legendary: faster than a speeding bullet, more powerful than a locomotive, able to leap tall buildings in a single bound! Another phrase attached to Superman is his one-sentence mission statement: To fight for truth, justice, and the American way.

That was obviously written to sum up our preferred reality— for truth to win, for justice to prevail, and for us all to experience the American dream. (Too bad, Canada—Superman isn't crossing the border without the Stars and Stripes.)

In the Amy Grant Christmas song "My Grown-up Christmas List," we hear the longings of an adult who still has wishes for a proverbial Santa. These are not for a doll or a toy or a hippopotamus, but rather things that embrace the new reality this grown-up is now facing, including peace between nations, healing for hearts, and that "right would always win."

Isn't that what we all want—justice?

It's most obvious when we feel that we are wronged.

Think about when you are in traffic. You're driving along, listening to worship music, singing along, praising God, then out of nowhere someone pulls in front of you and hits the brakes. It's amazing how quickly we can go from "I love you, Lord" to "You stupid jerk!" At that moment, the grace of Jesus we were just weeping over turns into our prayer for God to bring his mighty arm of wrath down upon this inconsiderate driver. Could God send a police officer at least?

How about when you go get your prescriptions filled and the pharmacist has to break the news to you that your insurance no longer covers this medicine. Suddenly what was supposed to cost you a ten-dollar co-pay is now going to cost you two hundred dollars. Our first reaction is to plead our case. "What am I supposed to do?" "How am I going to pay for that?" "Why would they not cover it?" All questions that the pharmacist is not equipped to answer, but we ask them anyway. We are wanting answers. We've been wronged. We want justice.

Think about something even more painful. Someone breaks your daughter's heart. A college rejects your son's admission request. An employer is harassing your wife. Your boss hires his inexperienced son rather than promoting you. Everything in you wells up with a desire for justice. *Fix this wrong, God.* Someone should know. Someone should do something.

We use whatever resources we have. If your child is being bullied, maybe you call the bully's parents. If your son can't get into college, you try to find out who you know who might know the academic dean. If your spouse is being harassed, you contact Human

Resources. If you're wrongfully passed over due to nepotism, you express your frustration. Maybe even quit.

We then take to the internet and use our voice to cry out for justice. We use our social media platforms as mediums for our revenge. *If I can't get your attention, if I can't fix this, then I'll just make your life miserable. I'll tell everyone how awful you are until they are crying out for justice against you as well.*

I once had an employee who every time he received any kind of instruction or correction, he would go home and complain to his wife about how unfairly he had been treated. How did I know this? Because she always shared their conversations and her feelings about it on Facebook! Always the perfect place for conflict resolution. She wanted justice. As defined by her.

Justice is not just declaring someone innocent. It is also declaring someone guilty. This woman was not just declaring the innocence and unfair treatment of her husband, she was condemning the behavior of his employers. Every time you and I cry out for justice, we seek it not just on the part of those wronged, but for action to be taken against the perpetrator. That's quite a decision to make. How do we know how to wield this judgment?

> Every time you and I cry out for justice, we seek it not just on the part of those wronged, but for action to be taken against the perpetrator.

When justice is only on our behalf, it's always for our benefit. That's why our view is always subjective. So what does it mean when Micah says this is what God wants of us . . . to "act justly"?

How the Bible Talks about Justice

To fully understand this, we need to go back to Abraham. After the flood and the repopulation of the world, God chose a family to not just begin his plan to save the world, but also as a model for how to treat others.

God tells Abraham,

> "I will make you into a great nation, and I will bless you; I will make your name great, and you will *be a blessing*."
>
> Genesis 12:2 (emphasis added)

I will bless you . . . I will protect you . . . but I do this so you will be a blessing to others. How does God do that? Through righteousness and justice.

The word for *righteousness* is an ethical standard that refers to "right" relationships between people. It is treating others with the God-given dignity they deserve.

Justice is the Hebrew word *mishpat,* and it can convey one of two separate meanings. The first is retributive. You have to pay the consequences for what you do wrong. If you steal something, you go to jail. An eye for an eye.

But most often in the Bible it refers to restorative justice. It means to go a step beyond just administering punishment or receiving it. It means seeking out those being taken advantage of and helping them. More than just charity, it means to advocate for the oppressed. It means to seek social structure changes to prevent this from happening again. It means to take whatever blessings you have received and make sure others can have that opportunity to be blessed as well.

Justice and righteousness were to bring about a whole new way of life.

A few generations after Abraham received this promise, his people began to see the value of because they no longer had it. They were oppressed by the Egyptians until God led them out of slavery. And even though God rescued them and renewed his covenant with them to be their God and to bless them to be a blessing, they turned around and began to oppress others.

Occasionally a king would rule Israel who would remember this. King David wrote this in regard to the blessing of God:

> He upholds the cause of the oppressed and gives food to the hungry. The Lord sets prisoners free, the Lord gives sight to the blind, the Lord lifts up those who are bowed down, the Lord loves the righteous. The Lord watches over the foreigner and sustains the fatherless and the widow, but he frustrates the ways of the wicked.
>
> Psalm 146:7–9

David's son, King Solomon, says this about what their response should be:

> Speak up for those who cannot speak for themselves, for the rights of all who are destitute. Speak up and judge fairly; defend the rights of the poor and needy.
>
> Proverbs 31:8–9

But as often happens, the oppressed, when they are free, become the oppressor. The good become the wicked. And that's where Israel ends up. God lets them be overtaken and exiled to neighboring nations. And then God sends prophets to help them wake up to their first call.

Jeremiah writes,

> This is what the LORD says: Do what is just and right. Rescue from the hand of the oppressor the one who has been robbed. Do no wrong or violence to the foreigner, the fatherless or the widow, and do not shed innocent blood in this place.
>
> Jeremiah 22:3

Isaiah writes startling words from God to his people as well:

"The multitude of your sacrifices—what are they to me?" says the Lord. "I have more than enough of burnt offerings, of rams and the fat of fattened animals; I have no pleasure in the blood of bulls and lambs and goats. When you come to appear before me, who has asked this of you, this trampling of my courts? Stop bringing meaningless offerings! Your incense is detestable to me. New Moons, Sabbaths and convocations—I cannot bear your worthless assemblies. Your New Moon feasts and your appointed festivals I hate with all my being. They have become a burden to me; I am weary of bearing them. When you spread out your hands in prayer, I hide my eyes from you; even when you offer many prayers, I am not listening. Your hands are full of blood! Wash and make yourselves clean. Take your evil deeds out of my sight; stop doing wrong. Learn to do right; seek justice. Defend the oppressed. Take up the cause of the fatherless; plead the case of the widow."

Isaiah 1:11–17

If those words were written today to the modern church, they might read

All of your church services . . . what are they to me? I have enough praise offerings, clap offerings, and Christmas offerings. I have no pleasure in your reading my book, arguing about what I meant, and calling yourself holy. I cannot bear your conferences and rallies that promote your platforms. Even though you think you are honoring me with your worship, you are neglecting those in need. You step over homeless people on your way to your cathedrals. You sing to me on Sunday but steal from your boss on Monday. You pray for a parking spot at the mall while children are being trafficked. Seek justice! Encourage the oppressed.

Something like that.

So when Micah comes around, he wants to call them back to their original mandate—to be blessed to be a blessing. And when he writes "act justly," he is not telling the people of Israel to begin wielding a subjective sword with no guidance whatsoever. Micah is directing their attention back to the Holiness Code established by God through Moses as recorded in Leviticus 17–26.

The children of Israel had been rescued from slavery and freed to establish a new life. God basically says to them, "We are in a covenant relationship with each other. You are my people and I am your God. Here are ten commandments to guide us." And in Leviticus he gets very specific on how these are applied.

Now, I know Leviticus seems to be a bit outdated and tedious. After all, how often have you meditated and received great strength from "Don't touch a gecko" (11:29)? But Micah is calling us back to its intent.

Dr. Jeremy Smoak states:

Ritual is empty without socio-economic justice and socio-economic justice is empty without ritual. The prophets loved ritual, but they railed against the idea that walking around the temple could save one. Too much of Protestant tradition has interpreted the prophets as if they were against ritual or somehow created a binary between ritual and faith. I think that that's wrong-headed. I think that Micah is espousing the virtues of the book of Leviticus, particularly 17–26, the same way that Jesus did. It is the Torah after all that defines holiness as the interweaving of justice and ritual holiness. I see Micah basically saying that Leviticus 19 is what the people are NOT obeying.[1]

> To "act justly" is to make sure that your neighbor is well taken care of, and to "love mercy" is to always be there for said neighbor.

What does Leviticus 19 say?

Leave some crops for those who are in need. Don't cheat people. Don't rob your neighbor. Pay people when it's payday. Don't take advantage of the poor and be partial to the rich. Judge fairly.

In a sentence: Love your neighbor as yourself.

Justice is courageously making other people's problems your problems. To "act justly" is to make sure that your neighbor is well taken care of, and to "love mercy" is to always be there for said neighbor, just as God is always there for us.

When Justice Goes Wrong

The prophet Amos comments on the misuse of justice:

> Do horses run on the rocky crags? Does one plow there with oxen? But you have turned justice into poison, and the fruit of righteousness into bitterness.
>
> Amos 6:12

We are not God, and our understanding of God is often limited and imperfect. So much so that even our own views of justice can actually do more harm than good. We have to have what Professor Miroslav Volf calls "double vision." In other words, learning to hold fast to our convictions and traditions while also learning and embracing people of different backgrounds, and yes, even those who have committed crimes or offenses.

> When we are looking at each other through the sights of our own guns we see only the rightness of our own cause. We think more about how to enlarge our power than to enlarge our thinking; we strive to eliminate others from our world, not to grant them space in ourselves. . . . *The will to embrace the unjust precedes agreement on justice.*[2]

Volf goes on,

> To agree on justice in conflict situations you must want more than justice; you must want embrace. *There can be no justice without the will to embrace.*[3]

Micah tells us to "act justly," to *do justice*. To do so is to know and walk with God. As Christine Caine says in her book *Undaunted*, "It's one thing to be awakened to injustice and quite another to be willing to be inconvenienced and interrupted to do something about it."[4]

So now that we are "awakened," each of us needs to figure out how to act justly. For one thing, we have to be "doers" of the Word, not just "hearers" (James 1:22 NASB). We constantly have to see our desire and struggle for justice through the eyes of other people, not ourselves. Why? Because that is also where we experience God the most. Love has to be at the center of everything we do, especially when we talk about justice.

I think this is where we miss it. Richard Rohr says that much of our social justice efforts are reflections of our personality.[5] Introverts are content to pray silently or sign petitions; extroverts will serve in homeless shelters and go on mission trips. Both think they are right and the other is either slacking off or overdoing it.

Pastor Larry Osborne once said that most of our passion for social justice is more than just personality; it is gift projection. So when Scripture states to take care of the widows and orphans, those with the gift of mercy want to serve them food. Those with the gift of hospitality want to bring them home. Those with the gift of administration want to organize a food drive. Those with the gift of leadership want to run for office. All good things. The problem comes when we think our way is the best way and the only way. The point is to bring justice for all and in all necessary ways.

How Jesus Did This

Jesus stated what this was all about when he answered the Pharisees' question regarding the greatest commandment.

Hearing that Jesus had silenced the Sadducees, the Pharisees got together. One of them, an expert in the law, tested him with this question: "Teacher, which is the greatest commandment in the Law?" Jesus replied: "'Love the Lord your God with all your heart and with all your soul and with all your mind.' This is the first and greatest commandment. And the second is like it: 'Love your neighbor as yourself.' All the Law and the Prophets hang on these two commandments."

Matthew 22:34–40

It all boils down to love of God and love of others.

How does this apply to justice?

I think this is what Jesus was saying when he stood up in the temple and declared who he was. Imagine going to temple every week with Jesus, and one day when he's about thirty he decides to stand up and read. And he doesn't read just any passage, he reads one that predicts the Messiah.

"The Spirit of the Lord is upon me, for he has anointed me to bring Good News to the poor. He has sent me to proclaim that captives will be released, that the blind will see, that the oppressed will be set free, and that the time of the Lord's favor has come."

Luke 4:18–19 NLT

As if that wasn't enough, he states, *"The Scripture you've just heard has been fulfilled this very day!"* Mic drop.

Not only does Jesus declare this, he lives it out. He lives among the poor, he tells them they are blessed and frees those oppressed by blindness and disease and death, and then he wields the sword of justice upon sin by falling on it. To act justly is to be among the poor, to fight for those who can't fight for themselves, to speak up for those who do not have a voice, and to speak out against their oppressors.

A Simple Way to Follow

Do you know anyone in need? How would THEY define justice? I know I would probably define it differently from someone in need. Perhaps their oppressor is more than their boss, it's their inability to get an education. How can we address that? Maybe their oppressor is their generational poverty and they keep striking out at interviews due to poor appearance, penmanship, and the inability to fill out an application. How can we help? Perhaps they have it all together and look like they have the world by the tail, but their oppressor is years of sexual abuse that keeps them haunted and running. How can we address that?

Following Jesus is simply this: making room in our hearts for other people on the narrow and humble path of life. That is the heart of discipleship. When we do so, it is not self-serving but benefits everyone we encounter and everyone we travel on this road with. This, conversely, turns out to be the most beneficial for us too. If our neighbor is happy, chances are we might be too. If we are heeding Jesus' call and actually praying for the well-being of our enemies, who's to say their well-being won't actually benefit us in return? Here, the cycle of retribution, vengeance, and wrath is rendered useless by mercy. This is humility.

> Following Jesus is simply this: making room in our hearts for other people on the narrow and humble path of life.

Jesus once said this in response to the lack of attentiveness of the people of God toward the justice of God: "Truly I tell you, the tax collectors and the prostitutes are entering the kingdom of God ahead of you" (Matthew 21:31). Justice can be surprising at times and look nothing like we define it, describe it, or do it. Luckily, Jesus shows us as good an example as there is.

That is truth, justice, and the kingdom's way.

TO-DO LIST

- If you are carrying resentment toward anyone, try forgiving them this week.
- If there is anyone that you have potentially wronged or caused injustice, reach out and reconcile with them by apologizing and asking forgiveness.
- Carve out time during the day or before you go to bed to intentionally pray for the well-being of someone who you are currently in an argument with, has done you wrong, or you even simply don't like. If you cannot think of a prayer, pray the Lord's Prayer on their behalf (Matthew 6:9–13).

DISCUSSION QUESTIONS

1. How do you recognize justice when you see it? Try and describe it if you can.
2. How do love and justice go together?
3. In what ways does your own personality naturally pursue justice? After reading this chapter, do you think that is actually helping or hurting?

seven

When Helping Is Hurting

We were new to California and were invited by some locals to try a Los Angeles landmark known for their French dip sandwiches. In fact, they even claimed to have invented them. Wouldn't that be an L.A. dip sandwich? What do I know? Philippe's is located in downtown L.A., and it took us about an hour to get there. We exited the freeway and began weaving through the concrete jungle of the inner city passing cardboard houses and panhandlers on the corner. As we pulled into the parking lot and opened the car doors, the smell of roast beef and fresh baked bread greeted us and called us inside. I could already tell this would be worth the drive.

Making our way to the front door, we were approached by a homeless man. He asked if we had any money we might be able to give him. He was trying to get a bus ticket back to his family in Kentucky, he offered. I can be a bit skeptical at times with people's stories. *Did he really have family in Kentucky? Is that actually what he would do with the money?* So I began to ask him some questions about where his family in Kentucky lived. We had lived there for several years and might be able to validate his story. But before I could finish my investigation, one of our friends pulled out a $20 and handed it to him. The gentleman was very grateful, and then walked over and hopped on a very nice bicycle and rode off down the road. This was a bit unsettling for my friend who had just ponied up the twenty. "Where'd he get the bike?" he wondered aloud. "Is he really going to Kentucky?" I began to nod along with his concerns, and just before I'm sure one of us was going to mention the possibility of using the money for drugs or alcohol, one of the women we were with spoke up and said, "Who cares what he does with it? That's on him. It was on you to give him the money!" I felt a bit ashamed that I didn't say that. After all, I was the pastor in the group. She was right. Or was she?

Is it enough to give and never take responsibility for what we may be funding?

Back when my wife and I were living in Kentucky and new in ministry, we were leading a college-age ministry. We decided to take a group of students on a mission trip to Florida. Yes, it did include a day at Disney World. We had to have a hook for the college students, and this seemed to do the trick. Part of the mission work was to connect with a local church and help meet some needs in their community. We were given the task of painting a family's house. Seemed easy enough. There were twenty of us and two large canisters of paint. What could go wrong?

Immediately we noticed that while the paint marked "House" was white, the paint marked "Trim"—though labeled *beige*—appeared to also be white. By the time the group doing the trim saw the color of the paint going on the house, it was already too late. Six hours later we had pretty much white-washed an entire home. It looked like the White House or a house in a snowstorm. To top it off, as we were cleaning up, I noticed that one of our team members had apparently asked to use the bathroom and tracked white paint into the house. It wasn't enough that the outside was white, the inside now had white footprints. We politely apologized, did our best to clean things up, took a picture with the family, and raced away in our church van!

As we drove away, I wondered, *Did we really make their life better? Was it enough that we painted it, even if it wasn't done well? Can the axiom "It's the thought that counts" really be enough?*

When Helping Others Is Just Helping Us

When we talk about justice for others, it is to be done with the benefit of others as the priority. Yet while we may be trying to alleviate their pain, often the only discomfort we alleviate is our own.

We all have seen a commercial of starving children and felt the pang of "I should do something." And in those rare moments we discovered that when the remote is too far and we can't change the channel, we are left with the bad taste in our mouth of our own comfort and privileged lifestyle. So we decide to do something. We sponsor a child, we send a check, we support an organization. And in that moment, we feel better. We have administered justice.

But is that all there is? What if our attempt at helping others is just to make ourselves feel better?

As mentioned in the previous chapter, there are people who assume all acts of justice must involve activist marches, the protection of rights, and the amending of laws. Those who serve anonymously assume that all acts of kindness and justice should be done from behind closed doors and with no one knowing it was you. So when they see people promoting their mission trip on Instagram, they assume they are arrogant. If the only way we define justice is by our preference, then our definition of justice is limited to our personality, and thus will only benefit us.

Not long after I arrived at Real Life Church, I came face-to-face with this exact situation. We were still meeting in a movie theater, and our offices were in a building in an older part of town. One day when I was leaving the office, there was a homeless woman sitting on our lawn. I asked her name and what she might need. She explained her situation and began telling me she had nowhere to go, nowhere to stay, and nothing to eat. I felt the shame of being a church and having nothing for her. I couldn't send her away. So I made arrangements for her to get a room at a nearby hotel, gave her some grocery money, and prayed for her. Surely this would be enough. As I made my way back into the office feeling like a good Samaritan, another pastor on staff asked me about what happened. I told him what I'd done, expecting a word of exaltation. Instead he cautioned me with, "She'll be back." And she was. The next day she needed more money and more housing. Even though I felt great about myself, I'm not sure I made her life any better.

When Helping Others Is Just Hurting Others

My family and I sponsor several children overseas, one of whom is a young girl from Uganda. I have been to visit her, and I brought gifts from my girls for her. We were cautioned about bringing too much and showering her with gifts. My thought was, *They're just trying to protect us from bringing too much and overindulging the children.* But I played by the rules and brought her some stickers and candy and a couple of books. This seemed to be acceptable.

After spending a week in her village, I could quickly see the needs that she had. Correct that, not needs—she had food, clothing, shelter, education, and a loving church community. What I saw she lacked were the creature comforts that my family was used to, like technology, sheets with a higher thread count, steady electricity, hot water, and amusement. So going home it was hard for me to not want to provide some of the "finer" things for her. When we would receive Christmas catalogs allowing us to purchase Christmas gifts for her, none of the above mentioned items were included. Instead we could buy her a chicken or a goat. Those seemed nice but too practical. But we obliged.

A few months later, in speaking with one of the board members of this organization, he told us there had been a problem at the orphanage. It seemed that some well-meaning visitors from the West had brought bigger gifts than just stickers and candy. Some children got gaming devices or technology, and one even got a bike! As thrilled as the receiving children were, others weren't so excited. "Why does your sponsor bring you that and I get stickers?!" In fact, the child with the bike was accosted one day going home from school, and the bike was stolen. I guess sometimes even when we mean well, our idea of gifts isn't always in their best interest.

The fear many of us have when helping others is that our generosity actually hinders them from helping themselves. How can our justice offer a hand up more than a handout?

We all fear that when we give twenty dollars to a guy on the street, we may be fueling an addiction or enabling a lifestyle. But

> **How can our justice offer a hand up more than a handout?**

what if that is possible even in our best and most vetted attempts?

One of the core differences in our country today can be seen in this very question. Lots of people are asking, "What is poverty, and what causes it?" One side says that poverty stems from problems in institutions and policies on a structural level. Others point more toward the personal behavior of individuals and place the blame there. What if the problem and the answer to addressing it actually lie on both sides? What if the answer to administering justice is both structural and behavioral? Furthermore, what can the church's role be in administering such justice on a local and global level?

Offering Help and Dignity

Consider this: Because God is a relational being, humans are as well. Specifically, in the course of human life, we relate to ourselves as individuals, to other human beings, to the world or creation, and to God. In short, people are created in the image of God and, therefore, are created to enjoy both personal freedom and communal relationship. Poverty, at its core, affects both of these aspects of human life.

Poor people typically talk in terms of shame, inferiority, powerlessness, humiliation, fear, hopelessness, depression, social isolation, and voicelessness. North American audiences tend to emphasize a lack of material things such as food, money, clean water, medicine, housing, etc.[1]

The prophet Isaiah states,

> If you spend yourselves in behalf of the hungry and satisfy the needs of the oppressed, then your light will rise in the darkness, and your night will become like the noonday.
>
> Isaiah 58:10

Spending yourself often involves more than giving a handout to a poor person—a handout that may very well do more harm than good.[2]

As has been mentioned, "justice" refers to so much more than just playing fair. If it were just fairness, justice would simply be about distributing material goods until everyone was satisfied. In other words, if only we could make the poor "rich," justice would be served. Instead, justice refers to so much more than material goods. Justice, if it is to be centered on the character and mission of God, has to include a community-centered focus. It has to be restorative of people's identity as children of God.

"Justice" refers to so much more than just playing fair.

In his book *Just Generosity*, Ronald Sider refers to four aspects of understanding a more biblically sound perspective of justice.

1. Frequently the words *love* and *justice* appear together in close relationship.
2. Biblical justice has a dynamic, restorative character.
3. The special concern for the poor running through Scripture moves beyond a concern for unbiased procedures.
4. Restoration to community—including the benefit rights that dignified participation in community require—is a central feature of biblical thinking about justice.[3]

These points can be applied in three different areas: the community of Israel in the Old Testament, the ministry of Jesus, and the mission of the church today. In all three, relationships are always the priority.

In the Old Testament, we read the epic story of the people of Israel. Israel is often referred to as the "chosen people" because God chose to work through them so that they could be a positive influence to the rest of the world and be a testament to the other nations of God's steadfast love. God describes them as holy, or set apart, so that they could be a blessing to everyone around them. As mentioned earlier, in Genesis 12:2 God tells Abraham, "I will make you into a great nation, and I will bless you; I will make your name great, and you will be a blessing."

One major way in which Israel was supposed to be such a blessing was through their concern for the poor. This is one of the main themes, especially throughout the prophets such as Micah. In the midst of social struggles within the different tribes of Israel, God takes initiative to make things better and expects his people to follow suit. This is also how we get such concepts as the Sabbath and "Jubilee," because God gave Moses this same vision to care for the poor.

Furthermore, the Sabbath guaranteed a day of rest for the slave (Exodus 23:10–12). The Sabbath year canceled debts for Israelites, allowed the poor to glean from the fields, and set slaves free as well as equipping the slaves to be productive (Deuteronomy 15:1–18). The Jubilee year emphasized liberty; it released slaves and returned land to its original owner (Leviticus 25:8–55). Other laws about debt, tithing, and gleaning ensured that the poor would be cared for each day of the year (Leviticus 25:35–38; Deuteronomy 14:28–29; Leviticus 19:9–10). The commands were so extensive that they were designed to achieve the ultimate goal of eradicating poverty among God's people: "There need be no poor people among you," God declared (Deuteronomy 15:4). After all, poor citizens in a kingdom reflect poorly on the king and his kingdom.[4]

However, the Israelites failed to live up to these expectations. Instead, many got rich off of the very people they were supposed to be taking care of. Thus, the prophets came along and told the people just how frustrated God was by this.

> Among my people are the wicked who lie in wait like men who snare birds and like those who set traps to catch people. Like cages full of birds, their houses are full of deceit; they have become rich and powerful and have grown fat and sleek. . . . They do not defend the just cause of the poor.
>
> Jeremiah 5:26–28

Because of this kind of neglect, prophets like Amos warned that God was so mad that he would destroy the nations of Israel and Judah and take them into captivity, or exile, because of how they "trample on the heads of the poor . . . and deny justice to the oppressed" (Amos 2:7). Many prophets, including Micah, predicted such a captivity, and we know now that they were right. We have a lot to learn from Israel's mistakes: If we get wealthy by means of making others worse off and don't care for the needy, God is not pleased. "God judges societies by what they do to the people at the bottom."[5]

These weren't just laws to be followed, these were guidelines for living faithfully to God. Love and justice are intertwined. You don't get one without the other. As Hosea puts it, "Sow righteousness for yourselves, reap the fruit of unfailing love" (Hosea 10:12). More than simply a material gift, justice often describes deliverance of people from politically and economically oppressive situations (Judges 5:11–12), slavery (1 Samuel 12:7–8, Micah 6:4), and captivity (Isaiah 41:1–11, Jeremiah 51:10). With these in mind, justice doesn't just teach people how to cope with bad situations in their life, it teaches us to try to remove those situations from their life entirely and restore them to their God-given inclination to *belong*.

Leviticus 25:35–36 puts it directly: "If any of your fellow Israelites become poor and are unable to support themselves among you, help them as you would a foreigner and stranger . . . so that they may continue to live among you." Not only are we to simply throw a bandage on a poor situation, we're called to empower those who are in such situations. It is so much more than a donation.

> Whoever is kind to the poor lends to the Lord.
>
> Proverbs 19:17

> Whoever oppresses the poor shows contempt for their Maker.
>
> Proverbs 14:31

How Jesus Did This

Jesus addressed this in his haunting story about the sheep and the goats as recorded in Matthew 25. Speaking of the hungry, sick, and alien, Jesus says, "Truly I tell you, whatever you did for one of the least of these brothers and sisters of mine, you did for me" (Matthew 25:40).

Food, shelter, clothing, yes. But what if the greatest resource we can provide costs us nothing but our time? And what if the gift of a listening ear is more valuable to someone than a twenty-dollar bill?

I think this is why we see Peter and John give gifts of healing and help without giving silver and gold. And while you and I may not be able to heal, we can help with our time, our care, our prayers, and in some cases our resources.

What if the greatest resource we can provide costs us nothing but our time?

In the Gospels we read that Jesus often sent out his disciples to do ministry, to "proclaim the kingdom of God and heal the sick" (Luke 9:2; see also Luke 10:9, etc.). Jesus talked a lot about the kingdom of God, and when he did, he wasn't just talking about another political power or government. When Jesus talks about the kingdom of God, he's referring to another way of living within the world, one that promotes peace, justice, and equality for all.

This really shows when Jesus did healings of his own. Whether he was healing a demonized person, sick person, blind person, lame person, ritually unclean person, or the like, when he did so, they received more than simply a physical benefit. Not only did Jesus see these people as human beings and legitimately cared for them as such; when he healed them, many of them were restored to community. When Jesus healed people, he wasn't just healing them physically, he was healing them spiritually and restoring them to access to the very community from which they were outcast because of their various conditions. Jesus saw people for what they were—children of God created in God's image—and he simply reminded them of that fact through healing them and restoring their ability to make an impact on the community around them.

Furthermore, Jesus calls his church to do the very same. One of the first descriptions we see of the early church after Jesus ascended into heaven was that "there were no needy persons among them" (Acts 4:34). This is a mirror image of what God was calling Israel to do in Deuteronomy 15:4, as we read earlier.

The goal is to see people restored to being what God created them to be: people who understand that they were created in the image of God with the gifts, abilities, and capacity to make decisions and effect change in the world around them; and people who steward their lives, communities, resources, and relationships in order to bring glory to God.[6]

A Simple Way to Follow

Offer what people need most: dignity.

It's a shame, but when many of us are moved to give to the poor, we do so under the motivation of making those we're giving to more like us. In other words, we think that being generous to people will make them more middle class on an economic level. But faith requires us to change this perspective.

What we can learn from Israel, and as we're about to see, Jesus, too, is that it is all about restoring a relationship. The mission and role of the church in the world today is simple: to do what Jesus did. Or, put another way, "to do justice, love mercy, and walk humbly with God." This seems simple enough, but it is so incredibly difficult because it requires an entire lifestyle of dedication and an entire lifetime of commitment to other people. It is so much more than a one-time donation. And particularly in North America, where capitalism is what most of us know best, it can require a major change in how we view and describe justice and poverty.

In their wonderful book *When Helping Hurts*, Steve Corbett and Brian Fikkert describe our response to poverty in three separate stages: relief, rehabilitation, and development. We provide immediate relief to a person's pain, we provide a method to get them more permanent care, but then we offer them a way to grow beyond their current state. Many of us are accustomed to focusing only on the first part when it comes to confronting poverty, whether it's giving twenty dollars to a homeless guy on the street or donating to the Red Cross every time there is a natural disaster. However, as they say in the book, "One of the biggest mistakes that North American churches make—by far—is in applying relief in situations in which rehabilitation or development is the appropriate intervention."[7] Is this really justice? Is this really what the Lord requires of us?

Sociologist Rodney Stark documents that the early church's engagement with suffering people was crucial to its explosive growth. Cities in the Roman Empire were characterized by poor sanitation, contaminated water, high population densities, open sewers, filthy streets, unbelievable stench, rampant crime, collapsing buildings, and frequent illnesses and plagues. "Life expectancy at birth was less than 30 years—and probably substantially less," Stark writes.[8] Rather than fleeing these urban cesspools, the early church found its niche there. Stark explains that the Christian concept of self-sacrificial love of others, emanating from God's love for them, was a revolutionary concept to the pagan mind, which viewed the extension of mercy as an emotional act to be avoided by rational people. Hence, paganism provided no ethical foundation to justify caring for the sick and destitute who were being trampled by the teeming urban masses.

> Christianity revitalized life in Greco-Roman cities by providing new norms and new kinds of social relationships able to cope with many urgent urban problems. To cities filled with the homeless and impoverished, Christianity offered charity as well as hope. To cities filled with newcomers and strangers, Christianity offered an immediate basis for attachments. To cities filled with orphans and widows, Christianity provided a new and expanded sense of family. To cities torn by violence and ethnic strife, Christianity offered a new basis for social solidarity. And to cities faced with epidemics, fires, and earthquakes, Christianity offered effective nursing services.[9]

I have yet to meet anyone experiencing homelessness that told me being homeless was their plan. In most cases, their situation is a result of broken relationships rather than a lack of resources. When we see them as a person with a story and a history—someone who is often wanting someone to merely look them in the eyes and truly see them, give them a smile, recognize them as a fellow human being and not some animal in a zoo—this simple act can be life-giving. If you feel compelled to give them some money, go ahead. If you have time to have coffee or share a meal, do that. Maybe you just have time to shake their hand and engage in a quick conversation. All of these offer more than a handout; they offer dignity.

Our outreach pastor, Steve Meyers, tells this life-changing story that happened in our church:

> One night after church, I helped one of our homeless friends get back to his "home." A tent. Before he got out of the car, he stopped and told me he had been listening to Rusty teach about stewardship and tithing, and he began to save up his tithe. He kept forgetting to drop it off in the offering bag and asked if I would take it and do that for him. He reached in his backpack and pulled out $245.62 . . . and then asked if I would pray for the offering. We both bowed our heads in my Jeep and I cried my way through the prayer. All the way back to church I thanked God for my friend Mike and the lesson of generosity and faithfulness I learned.

When we engage in genuine relationship, change happens on both sides. Real transformation happens.

I saw this recently at an evening hosted by our church to feed the hungry on the street. My family and I went to watch and learn and serve. We showed up to a well-run organization helping people get a hot meal, resources for the week, free haircuts, and even clothes. But that was not all. The volunteers showed up and offered friendship. They sat with people, they asked questions, they talked about life, and they prayed for them. For two hours on a Monday night we met not only physical needs, but also emotional. I saw executives who had six-figure salaries sitting with people who had six dollars to their name . . . and they formed a bond of friendship. I saw educators serve dessert to the mentally ill and provide a listening ear. And while some needs were met, the greater gift given was dignity and love. No one requested a car or a job or the equivalent to a lottery ticket, but they received dignity, confidence, and some supplies to help get them back on their feet. That always helps and never hurts.

TO-DO LIST

- Smile, say hello, even ask the name of a homeless person and strike up a conversation. A little goes a long way.
- Make a couple of resource kits to keep handy in your vehicle for when you encounter someone in need. Here are a few items to include:

  - ☐ $10 gift card to local eatery
  - ☐ Dry, nonperishable snacks
  - ☐ Socks
  - ☐ Underwear
  - ☐ Sunscreen
  - ☐ Hard candy
  - ☐ Bottle of water
  - ☐ New T-shirt
  - ☐ Fleece blanket
  - ☐ Reading material/Bible
  - ☐ Travel-size toothpaste
  - ☐ Toothbrush
  - ☐ Deodorant

- Commit to sponsoring a child from Compassion International for a year at compassion.com/sponsor.
- Partner with International Justice Mission by

  ☐ Advocating with your local or state representative
  ☐ Writing an encouraging letter to IJM field staff
  ☐ Becoming a "Freedom Partner" for $25/month
  ☐ See all these options at ijm.org

DISCUSSION QUESTIONS

1. When you encounter someone who asks you for money, do you tend to be more permitting or skeptical? Why do you think this is?
2. What "types" of people do you stereotype the most and struggle to see as someone in need, or more, a child of God?
3. It was mentioned in this chapter that justice is more than a distribution of material things. Is that a new concept to you? Does it paint a bigger picture of justice for you? How so?

eight

Self-Justice

I was probably fifteen when I felt the need to administer some justice.

My buddy and I were up late at my house, trying to think of something fun to do, when the thought occurred to us—we should go TP someone's house! For those of you unfamiliar with the term, it means "to apply toilet paper liberally to someone's lawn, trees, and house without them knowing." Some may call this rolling, others may call it a misdemeanor—we called it a great time. And we knew just the victim. A "frenemy" from down the street. This would be good for him. So our sense of justice thought.

There are several variations on TP-ing. "Forking" involves sticking plastic forks—tine-side up—all over the yard. I've heard of some who dump dog food all over the lawn. I even heard of one creative genius who sprinkled instant mashed potatoes all over the lawn, and when the sprinklers went off . . . voila! Just add gravy. Either way, this is an awful juvenile prank that I don't encourage. (At least on my house!)

So there we were, scavenging all the toilet paper from inside my house, opting out on the forks, dog food, and mashed potatoes, when a thought occurred to me: *We have a huge bag of beanbag pellets*. This was the 1980s, when beanbags were a big deal, and we not only had a few beanbags, we had replacement pellets. A huge bag of teeny, tiny Styrofoam pellets. This would be perfect to dust all over the lawn.

We crept out of the house like a team of Navy Seals. Down the street, around the corner, our paths lit by only the moon and streetlights. Armed with ten rolls of toilet paper and a giant bag of beanbag beans, we were in stealth mode. This was deep special ops. Fifteen short minutes later we declared the operation to be a huge success. The toilet paper draping the trees was beautiful in the moonlight. And the distribution of the beans lay on the ground like a blanket of new fallen snow. No one came outside. No one even turned on a light. No cars drove by. This mission was flawless.

We walked home laughing and high-fiving each other at our accomplishment. We envisioned their reaction the next morning at this epic event, and what sweet justice it would be. The recipient of our actions had been less of a friend to us over recent weeks. He'd abandoned us for other friends of ill repute. This would surely show him the error of his ways. God must have been applauding at how we had administered his justice. Or so we thought.

The next morning, after my partner in crime had gone home and it was just me, I really needed someone to gloat to. Like most criminals, I felt the need to let someone know what I had done—this was too good of a job to keep to myself. The problem was the only person who was around was my mother. But she knew of the lack of friendship I'd been experiencing with this particular neighbor, so I thought she'd enjoy this story.

As you may have assumed, she did not.

In fact, my assumptions were so far off that I didn't see her next words coming: "You need to go clean it up."

"What?! Are you kidding? I'll be caught; it'll be embarrassing. It will bring shame upon the family! Mom, surely you wouldn't want that on your only son!"

She didn't seem concerned by that.

I'll never forget ringing that doorbell, looking the family in the eye, and saying the words, "I'm sorry. I'm the one who TP'd your yard. I'm here to clean it up." They were shocked and hesitantly grateful. Taking down the toilet paper was not so hard, it was the beans that gave me trouble. I brought over a lawn mower to serve as a vacuum, and after a few trips around the yard, it got most of it. But while the yard may have been restored, my pride had been crushed. This was clearly not my view of justice.

Deciding how to administer justice can be a difficult feat.

We can find a way to "act justly" when we see someone in need and we can fix it. A broken system that can be corrected to alleviate pain. Equal hiring rights. Equal pay. Someone who is in need but is unable to get the resources to fend for themselves. This is why micro loans are so thrilling for us. It's not just a handout; it's a loan to change their life, and then they pay us back. What a great thing for us to be able to do. And it's clear for us to see how to be just.

We can even find a way to administer discipline and punishment as a form of justice for those who have been oppressed. It might be enforcing a time-out to your two-year-old because he took a toy from his younger sister. Or it might be seeking imprisonment for someone arrested for human trafficking. It might be hard, it might be easy, but we often know the right thing to do.

But there is one person to whom we find it hard to administer justice: ourself. How does one act justly to him or herself?

Poor Ways We Try to Justify Ourselves

"They deserved it."

In my mind, this individual down the street had it coming. *You should have heard what he said about me at school. If you heard my story, you'd agree with me. Toilet paper in the tree was a light sentence. He deserved so much more.*

And you have your story too. You may not have TP'd anyone, but you have decided to stop talking to them, administer the cold shoulder. Maybe you've handed out the sentence of "no longer worthy of my attention" to a few people. Maybe you've leveraged a few "let me tell you what they did" on Facebook. Perhaps you even tried to get them fired or tried to sue them. And maybe they deserved it. But it's hard to know for sure, isn't it? Justice is a sword that is difficult to know how hard to swing. And if this is the one we go with, we hardly ever leverage this type of justice on ourselves.

"They didn't care."

What I did wasn't even a crime! I get this a lot when my wife and I leave dinner parties. The debrief in the car often goes like this: "That was fun." "Yes, it was." "You really should apologize to him." "For what?" "You made a joke about his receding hairline." My response is always the same. "He doesn't care! He was laughing!" "You should still send a text to him." So I do, and the response is often a solemn "Thank you," not, "Don't worry about it." Self-justice is hard.

But some of us go to the other extreme.

"I'm worthless and I deserve any punishment I get."

Call it what you want—abandonment issues, low self-esteem, Eeyore syndrome—the truth is, there are a lot of us who don't know when to cry "uncle" to our own personal penance.

We may sin against someone, we say an errant word, we make an impulse decision that hurts others or just overlook someone, and we feel the world crashing in around us. We were responsible for their happiness, and now we have failed them. How can we ever recover from this?

I've struggled with this. When left to my own self-justice, the judge in my head says repeatedly, "Rusty is responsible. And Rusty is lacking." (My inner voice is very specific.) And so to pay the punishment I sentence myself to wallowing in self-pity, over-apologizing, or finding gifts to send and prove my worth, or if these aren't received, I resort to journaling about my own sinful soul. As Paul said, "Oh, wretched man that I am!"

> Some of us are good at rendering judgment on others but fail to hold ourselves to the same standards. And yet others are far too hard on themselves.

Some of us are good at rendering judgment on others but fail to hold ourselves to the same standards. And yet others are far too hard on themselves. How does the Father lead you to act justly to yourself?

Harvard Business Review shared this interesting depiction of four archetypes of self-awareness:[1]

Introspectors. *"They're clear on who they are but don't challenge their own views or search for blind spots by getting feedback from others. This can harm their relationships and limit their success."*

Think of how this impacts our view of self-justice. We tend to not even notice where our views might be wrong. We don't listen to anyone else, so our version of justice is just what is good with us.

I know my weaknesses, but they tend to be different from what my wife thinks. Apparently my tone and my face don't always communicate the kindness I may feel in my heart. Occasionally my wife will say, "That sounded mean." To which I respond, "But I'm not mad." "But your face and tone say something else," she replies. Even though I've done a lot of self-introspection and awareness tests and know that I'm punctual and a bit of a perfectionist, the reality is that my list of struggles stops there. If I'm going to act justly toward myself, I need others' input.

Think about King David. A shepherd and a poet first. All the long nights on the range watching sheep, studying the stars, playing songs on his harp for God. If anyone was introspective it was him. Look at these words . . .

"What is mankind that you are mindful of them." (Psalm 8:4)

"The Lord is my shepherd." (Psalm 23:1)

"The earth is the Lord's." (Psalm 24:1)

"By the word of the Lord the heavens were made." (Psalm 33:6)

And yet, when David sees a woman bathing next door, he sends his messengers for her and sleeps with her. When she becomes pregnant, he has her husband killed, takes her as his wife, and assumes everyone is none the wiser. Staggering how one of the most introspective and God-fearing men that ever lived is able to compartmentalize his morality, and hides this act away in the basement of his soul.

> Self-justice means being able to hear honesty about our reality.

But once the prophet Nathan confronts him, David is overwhelmed with grief and guilt.

Have mercy on me, O God. . . . Wash away all my iniquity. . . . Do not cast me from your presence. . . .

Psalm 51:1, 2, 11

At least he was able to listen to reason; most of us aren't. Self-justice means being able to hear honesty about our reality.

Seekers. *"They don't know who they are, what they stand for, or how [others] see them. As a result, they might feel stuck or frustrated with their performance and relationships."*

This person's self-justice is not based on how they see themselves or how others see them, they are looking for some sort of moral anchor.

We see this in the tax collector named Zacchaeus. He was a scoundrel with no scruples about swindling his own countrymen for the chance at getting rich. Yet he winds up going out to see Jesus. Why is he headed out there? He can't see anything, he's too short. He's not there to socialize, no one likes him. He's there to see the rabbi, the teacher, the miracle worker. He's looking for something. Some sort of meaning, purpose, hope.

In the words of the rock band Carolina Liar, "Save me, I'm lost . . . show me what I'm looking for."

Pleasers. *"They can be so focused on appearing a certain way to others that they could be overlooking what matters to them. Over time they tend to make choices that aren't in service of their own success and fulfillment."*

Apparently, Paul had a few instances when he came into contact with pleasers:

> Am I now trying to win the approval of human beings, or of God? Or am I trying to please people? If I were still trying to please people, I would not be a servant of Christ.
>
> Galatians 1:10

I've been there. And those of us who struggle with this end up with this self-abusive form of self-justice. We are at the whim of every opinion. "You should talk more." "You should listen more." "You should smile more." "You should offer to help." As my friend Dr. John Walker says, we let people "should" all over us.

Now, the fourth stage is the stage that *Harvard Business Review* tells us we need to move toward:

Aware. *"They know who they are, what they want to accomplish, and seek out and value others' opinions. This is where leaders begin to fully realize the true benefits of self-awareness."*

Take it easy on yourself. You are your own worst critic.

Be honest with who you are. You are the most just with yourself when you are the most self-aware.

"You get thirty minutes to be crazy."

Dr. John Walker, as mentioned before, has given me sage advice in this area. He once told me when I was in a pit of self-loathing, "Snap out of it. You get thirty minutes to be crazy."

So for all of you who tend to bring down the gavel on yourself rather quickly, set the clock for thirty minutes. Wail on yourself. Feel bad. Grovel. Say you're sorry. And then move on.

That being said, there are some things you just can't get over in a day. The verse "Don't let the sun go down on your anger" is less about "Say you're sorry before you go to bed" and more of "Get it right before this 'season' of your life is done." Don't carry your single-hood problems and mistakes into your marriage. Don't carry your family of origin issues into your family of marriage. In those cases of deep pain and grievances, it may take more than thirty minutes.

But for most things, confess and move on.

But let me add this to the thirty-minute rule: For those who are slow to bring the gavel down on yourself, when someone tells you that you may have overstepped your bounds . . .

Take Thirty Minutes to Reflect

Maybe they are right. Maybe you were out of line. Maybe they heard it differently than you meant. And perhaps they know exactly what you can do to make things right.

In either case, there is something to be said about self-justice and Micah. However, self-justice cannot come without first looking within ourselves. This is something that our culture isn't often accustomed to doing. We're either right, or the other person is wrong, right? Not so fast.

In a wonderful article published in *Christianity Today*, Professor Mark Gignilliat gives the challenge that he believes Micah gives us all, and that is to "walk reflectively."[2] In the article, he gives an illustration from the famous Hannah Arendt article chronicling the trial of Adolf Eichmann. Arendt was a German Jewish political theorist who had to flee Germany with her family during the rise of the Nazi regime. In the 1960s, she wrote a book entitled *Eichmann in Jerusalem: A Report on the Banality of Evil*, covering the trial of Adolf Eichmann, who was often called the "Architect of the Holocaust" because during World War II, he was in charge of the logistical side of deporting millions of Jewish people first into ghettos and, eventually, into concentration camps. After the war, when most German officers and war criminals were put on trial, Eichmann escaped to Argentina and lived under a different name for a while. Now a nation of their own, Israel found his whereabouts and captured Eichmann and took him back to Jerusalem for trial. Arendt covered the trial basically because she wanted to see the face of evil up close and personal.

Eichmann, she thought, must be a deranged, psychopath-looking killer. However, when she first laid eyes on him, she described him as normal-looking, rather polite, and not overly intelligent. He was, by all accounts, pretty shallow. She writes in the book, "Everybody could see that this man was not a 'monster,' but it was difficult indeed not to suspect that he was a clown."[3] So what prompted him to construct one of the most horrific and murderous tragedies in history? Duty. Over and over again, Arendt says that Eichmann's defense was that he was simply "doing [his] job." The problem was, he was doing it without question or hesitation no matter what order he was given. Gignilliat argues that this is the exact sort of thing that Micah is rallying against in Israel: an unreflective, shallow faith that doesn't walk the walk and always goes with the crowd or the boss.

In Micah 6, the people of Israel were losing their identity and forgetting who they were as God's chosen people. "Walking humbly with God" requires some work. As we've noted earlier, "humble" doesn't seem to get at the root of what is being said. Gignilliat notes that Gerhard von Rad, an Old Testament scholar, suggests the term is better translated as "measured, discerning, or circumspect." Whereas strutting involves walking without depth, walking humbly involves walking reflectively.

Every once in a while we're all prone to strutting around and living a shallow sort of life—doing what we're told, what we think others would want, even what we, ourselves, want. But Micah 6:8 calls us to reflect on the things we're doing and the things we hold most dear without conviction. This is where justice needs to be served to ourselves.

In other words, we're unwilling to admit that at times, when we call for justice, we need only to look in the mirror and start with ourselves. Michael Jackson–style. Make that change.

How Jesus Did This

Have you ever heard the word *zeitgeist*? It's a German word that means something like "spirit of the age." Every person succumbs to the spirit of their age, the zeitgeist, in some form or another. Richard Beck connects this to "drinking the Kool-Aid," referencing the Jim Jones cult members who drank Kool-Aid mixed with cyanide in order to "protest" an inhumane world and die with dignity. He writes, "The followers of Jones did not question the

Zeitgeist of the cult. Eichmann didn't question the Zeitgeist of Germany. And we fail to question the Zeitgeist of our own time and place."[4]

We've lost the ability to actually be critical of ourselves and the ways in which our lives and the ways we live them may be inflicting harm to others. When we're unable to do this, when we are unable to walk reflectively with God, but when we still call for justice regardless, it is as though we're TP-ing our own yard. But there is good news, and it is this:

> You see, at just the right time, when we were still powerless, Christ died for the ungodly. Very rarely will anyone die for a righteous person, though for a good person someone might possibly dare to die. But God demonstrates his own love for us in this: While we were still sinners, Christ died for us.
>
> Romans 5:6–8

We're all sinners, we all come up short, and we've all been conditioned by our culture in negative ways. But if we are going to start imagining and creating an alternative, it has to start with ourselves. It has to start by walking reflectively and walking the way of Micah, the way that leads to walking the way of Jesus. We must be able to step back and make a conscious choice to put ourselves on the stand, because when we don't, we run the risk of succumbing to "the banality of evil." In her last work, Hannah Arendt picks back up on the themes she covered in the Eichmann trial. Her words ring for us today: "The sad truth is that most evil is done by people who never make up their minds to be good or evil."[5] We need to make up our minds to act justly. Even unto ourselves.

While Jesus never needed to offer self-justice, he certainly spent time in self-reflection and assessment of his humanity. After the death of John the Baptist, he takes time to retreat in a boat to reflect. Certainly he had to process his cousin's death, the mortality of man, and the next steps in his mission. We read of Jesus taking a quiet moment at the funeral of Lazarus to weep for him, and the sting of death on all those mourning the loss of their friend and family member. Even though he knew he'd soon call Lazarus out of the tomb, he was overcome with his own emotions. But perhaps the most notable self-reflection Jesus had was in the Garden of Gethsemane, when we see him cry out to God for any other possible way to save the world. Here Jesus comes face to face with his own humanity and mortality.

A Simple Way to Follow

Here's the ironic thing about self-justice, though: It cannot be administered on our own. Like other aspects of following Jesus, as we've seen in the last couple chapters, justice is best done in community, because that is also where grace abounds. If we are truly "walking reflectively," or "walking humbly," whatever may be the case, then we are walking hand in hand with others on the road of life. This is where our faults, defects, and shortcomings come to light and are exposed; otherwise, how would we know they're there? Sometimes we need another person in our life to tell us to go clean it up when we make a mess of things.

Jesus came to save us, not only as individuals, but as a group, together. And one of the main ways in which our relationship with ourselves has been healed is through that very fact. Being in community with other people sets the stage for how we walk the rest of our lives and how we follow Jesus.

Convinced you need to have a healthy dose of self-justice? Immerse yourself within the local church. Form relationships that can hold you accountable, encourage you when you fall short, and love you even when you cannot love yourself. And likewise, be able to be that kind of community for somebody else.

TO-DO LIST

- If you aren't a part of one already, join a small group at your local church and start living life with others.
- Consider attending a twelve-step group or finding a church in your area that offers "Celebrate Recovery."
- Consider calling up a close friend and establishing an accountability relationship where you share life with one another and give one another permission to speak justly into each other's lives.

DISCUSSION QUESTIONS

1. Are you the kind of person who resorts to pointing the finger or absorbing the blame? Why do you think this is?
2. Out of the four self-awareness archetypes mentioned in this chapter, which one do you most identify with? How can you broaden your self-awareness to walk more reflectively?
3. Say your boss is asking you to do something shady, or a friend is asking a favor that could threaten the reputation of others or even yourself. Where would you draw the line between doing your duty and also acting justly in these types of situations?
4. What are some of the zeitgeists of our own time, and how can the notion of self-justice address them directly?

Step 3

↓

LOVE MERCY.

nine

For Those We Know and Love

"Oh mercy, mercy me. Things aren't what they used to be."
Mercy! Land sakes alive!
Mercy me.

What is mercy?

As a kid, there was a simple rule when roughhousing and wrestling with friends. If you are clearly beat, if you are pinned to the ground, if someone is asserting their will on you in some childish yet painful way, the way to get them to stop was to say "Mercy." Some would say "Uncle," but that never made sense to me. What does my uncle have to do with it? Our safe word was *mercy*, and it was always honored.

Growing up we learn that mercy is the ceasing of pain. So what does Micah mean when he says God's call for us is to "love mercy"?

At first glance, we may think that to love mercy is simply to approve of mercy. Or to cheer it on. We think of Jean Valjean in the play *Les Misérables* and the mercy he received that changed his life forever. We love that mercy. Every now and then we will hear of a tragic story of a tourist in a foreign land being arrested or detained. Our government goes to work on their behalf, and when we see their release we are thrilled. The news covers this and we watch their tearful return home and reunion with loved ones. We nod. We approve. We may even tear up. Mercy was given.

These stories can be closer to home. Maybe you've seen a co-worker allowed to keep their job after they big-time failed their project. Perhaps you've seen a friend forgive an ex-spouse for years of infidelity. We even see it with our children, when their teacher lets them make up a test, or when our kids grant mercy to one another for a disparaging remark or a clear violation. . . . We "love mercy."

But is mercy more than that?

The word Micah uses for "mercy" here is *hesed*, which is best summed up as "loving-kindness." This was a term that described God's kindness extended to his people, and thus the kindness his people are to extend to each other. But is that it?

What I find interesting is that most translations refer to it as "steadfast love." This is often aligned with the Greek word *agape*, which is an unconditional love. The best English translation is probably "faithfulness" or "commitment."

This word depicts what we think of when we see how God deals with his children, the Israelites. They cry out because they are enslaved, and he delivers them. Mercy. They complain because he brought them to the Red Sea and they were about to die; then he parted the sea. Mercy. They complained because they had nothing to eat; he gave them manna every morning. Mercy. They get bored with the sweetbread, so he gives them quail. Mercy. This is the kind, faithful, unconditional mercy that *hesed* encapsulates.

In fact, in the Old Testament, the word *hesed* is used most often for two relational situations: those you know, and those you don't know.

And it turns out there is a big difference between how we extend this type of kind, faithful mercy based on the nature of our relationships. But it's important we extend it to those we know as well as those we don't. "The refugee in Syria doesn't benefit more if you conserve your kindness only for her and withhold it from your neighbor who's going through a divorce."[1]

For Those We Don't Know

These are people we come across who we have no apparent reason to be generous or merciful to. You have no prior relationship with them, but you nevertheless act generously or mercifully by remaining faithful or committed to them. It's a five-dollar bill to the guy on the corner with a cardboard sign. It's letting someone go in front of you at the stop sign. You don't know them, they probably won't ever repay you, but you give them this gift of mercy. Or in another word, you give them the same kind of mercy and grace that the children of Israel received from God over and over again. And even the people who weren't part of the nation of Israel.

Even though God "knows" all, in the Old Testament his covenant was only with the nation of Israel, yet you see him extending mercy to those not in this tribe. Most notably is Rahab. Here is a woman who lives in Jericho, a city that God has just instructed the Israelites to go and wipe out. They were an abomination to God and to his people. Rahab is not only a citizen of this place, she is a prostitute—another character we did not have a flannel-graph for in my Sunday school class. Yet when Joshua and Caleb come to town to scout out the city, she gives them safe passage and hides them till they can safely escape. So God grants her his mercy. When the Israelites storm the city, she is spared. *Hesed . . .* for those not part of our tribe.

We'll talk about this more in the next chapter.

For now, let's look at the other way this kind, faithful mercy is extended.

For Those We Know

These are our friends. Our family. Our co-workers. Our crazy cousin and the brother-in-law of whom we do not speak. We know these people, we work with these people, we even like some of these people. And sometimes they are in need of help, encouragement, assistance, or even forgiveness. Perhaps they have hurt us or betrayed us in some way. Maybe they owe us an apology for a car they totaled or a Christmas vacation they ruined. Whatever the case, if in spite of what they owe you, you refuse to let this end the relationship, and instead you grant them kind, faithful, recurring mercy . . . that's the type of generosity God has modeled for us in his relationship with the Israelites.

God not only grants this to the nation of Israel when they first leave Egyptian slavery, but he also continues this pattern over and over again through the period of the Judges.

The children of Israel were led by Moses, then by Joshua, and then by judges appointed by God. But this begins a three-hundred-plus-year pattern of God's people disobeying . . . then facing the consequences . . . then God giving them mercy.

> Whenever the Lord raised up a judge for them, he was with the judge and saved them out of the hands of their enemies as long as the judge lived; for the Lord relented because of their groaning under those who oppressed and afflicted them. But when the judge died, the people returned to ways even more corrupt than those of their ancestors, following other gods and serving and worshiping them. They refused to give up their evil practices and stubborn ways.
>
> Judges 2:18–19

These people had a pull toward evil. They were easily distracted and enamored by the gods of neighboring countries. Sure, these gods had never delivered their people from Egyptian rule, these gods had never parted the Red Sea, nor had they provided manna and quail in the desert, but they did allow prostitution as acts of worship. So for some reason these people were easily persuaded. I'm so glad that we've grown beyond that!

So God would allow them to feel the full weight of his justice and their consequences. But when they would cry "uncle," God would step in with mercy. Kind, faithful, and compassionate. He would rescue them and appoint a new judge to lead them. And over three centuries they would obey, then rebel, then suffer, then cry uncle, and God would use a total of fifteen judges to bring them mercy.

Time and time again he continues to act justly, but then show mercy. Why does he do this? Because this is who God is, and this is who he asks us to be.

Granting kind, faithful mercy to those who are closest to us should be easy. After all, some of these people we are talking about are loved ones. It's easy to grant mercy to our kids. We have to fight to NOT give too much mercy at times. It's easy to grant mercy to those who can bless us. For instance, we tend to let our boss have a pass for jumping on our back, because we know they sign our paychecks. We even tend to let people we feel like we know have mercy—for instance, an athlete who plays for our favorite team or an actor of our favorite show. We feel like we know them, so when they make a mistake, when they miss a game-winning shot or are accused of unjust acts in the press, we cut them some slack because they make our lives better. Mercy to those we know or even feel like we know should come easy.

But not every time.

Sometimes the hardest to grant kind, faithful compassion and grace toward are those we know the best. Because no one can hurt us like a friend.

I've had anonymous people leave the church because they didn't like me or were mad at us for something we did or didn't do. And their words stung. But it's nothing compared to the words of a friend; they cut deep.

Maybe for you it was a trusted friend who sent a negative text about you to someone else but didn't realize you were on the group chat. Your first thought is not justice or mercy, it's "ouch."

Maybe for you it was a co-worker who stole your ideas, took credit for your work, and got the promotion that you felt was yours. What do you say the next time you see them?

Perhaps in your situation it was a spouse. They promised forever, but then you found out they were cheating on you. When you confronted them they were not repentant and contrite, but rather harsh and distant and blamed you for their lack of love at home and their need to look elsewhere. How can you ever trust again? Mercy for them? What about the kids? Are you kidding? How about mercy for me!

The words of Micah are interesting in their translation to love mercy. It's this idea of "I want mercy for you," "I celebrate when you get mercy," and "I love to give mercy to others." But how can we do that when the one who needs it most seemingly deserves it the least? After all, they were a trusted part of your world.

As always, Jesus models it for us best.

How Jesus Did This

When Jesus first met Peter, Peter was a rough-mouthed, hard-living fisherman who had given up on religion and was pursuing the family trade. And when Jesus helps him catch more fish than he'd ever seen and Peter decides to leave it all behind and follow Jesus, they quickly become fast friends.

Yet despite being a Jesus follower, Peter continues to say and do some pretty reckless things.

One day Jesus is with his disciples and he asks them, "Who do you say that I am?" They all hem and haw a bit with various answers, but it is Peter who steps up and says, "I think you are the Christ. The Son of God." Right answer, Peter! And Jesus commends him with, "On this rock I will build my church!" This is the guy who confessed earlier to having a dirty mouth. Jesus loves mercy.

Yet not long after this, Jesus will begin telling people of how he will soon have to die. Peter steps up, thinking he's saying the right thing, and declares, "This will never happen." To which Jesus says, "Get behind me, Satan." Seems like Jesus administers some justice by putting Peter in his place!

On another occasion Jesus will walk on water by a boat filled with the disciples. Peter will come out to join Jesus. And after taking a few steps he starts to sink. Jesus helps him. Mercy. Jesus corrects him. "Why did you doubt?" Justice.

The most memorable of all is the time when Peter denies Jesus outside in the courtyard near where Jesus is on trial. Three times people claim Peter knew Jesus, and three times Peter says, "I never knew him." After the resurrection, Jesus and Peter have some unfinished business. Justice, if you will. And sure enough Jesus asks Peter a piercing question: "Do you love me?" and what makes this so painful is he asks it three times. One for each denial. Peter responds "Yes" each time, but the justice has been clear. Then, in a strange twist, Jesus commissions Peter back with his original calling to build the church. Or "Feed my sheep." Mercy.

> God wants us to act decisively in a way that shows faithfulness to people just as God does to us.

Jesus is modeling how mercy can put a nuance on justice. We act justly so we can show mercy. God wants us to act decisively in a way that shows faithfulness to people just as God does to us.

A Simple Way to Follow

What can we learn from Jesus on how to show mercy to those we trust the most and thus hurt us the most?

Mercy is not commending. At no point does Jesus say, "What you did was right." Or even, "I get it, we all make mistakes." He acknowledges what was wrong. He calls it out. Then he offers mercy. You can still play in my sandbox.

Mercy is not forgetting. Jesus had not forgotten what Peter had done. He addressed it. And then moved on. Granting mercy to someone in your life allows the relationship to continue, but it may take time for you to forget what has happened. If ever. A wife who forgives her husband for an affair is merciful enough to allow the marriage to continue, but will find it hard to forget what has happened. And while the Father, Son, and Holy Spirit are able to forget, we may not be able to. Jesus models for us here that sometimes it's good to remember so we can address it and deal with the grievance.

Mercy is not just for their sake. When you grant someone mercy, it always impacts more than just the person who receives it. Sometimes the recipient is you. Even though you have let them off the hook by giving mercy, you feel a weight lifted because you are not carrying this weight anymore. It can be exhausting to always be reminding yourself who you are mad at and why. Letting that burden go can be life-giving to you as well.

> It can be exhausting to always be reminding yourself who you are mad at and why. Letting that burden go can be life-giving to you.

In some ways, mercy is like forgiveness. Forgiveness is a legal term. It's like saying, "You don't owe me anymore. Paid in full." Mercy is more like a medical term. "Let me offer healing for what it is you have done."

Sometimes the recipient is you, sometimes mercy is for others unrelated to your issue. In Peter's case, he received mercy, but the beneficiary was more than just him. It was the church. Because of this mercy and recommissioning from Jesus, he was able to stand up in front of thousands on the day of Pentecost and preach the gospel, and the church was born. This mercy was multiplied to countless others. We never know how the mercy we extend will impact more than just those immediately involved.

In a sentence, to love mercy is to extend kindness and compassion whether they deserve it or not.

One of the clearest expressions of mercy I've ever seen came in the home of a family I met many years ago.

Their college-age daughter I'll refer to as Donna, came to me, her college-age pastor, and said that her father had sexually abused her for five years. In some ways this girl had many of the signs of shame, recluse, and distance that made her story believable, but in other ways her story was shocking. Her father was a leader in the church I was serving, and this seemed to be far from his character, but I did as I should. I took her story seriously.

Over the next six months we began a painstaking process of her sharing her story with other trusted pastors and counselors, all of whom urged her of the need to confront her father. After all, she had a teenage sister who was still in the house. When it came to this, Donna became hesitant; she was unsure if she wanted to do this. But after a while she agreed. So a group of elders and pastors went to confront her father, while I and two other pastors went to talk to Donna's mom and sister. We sat down in a quiet room with tissues on the table and began to break the news to them about Donna's claims. They were horrified. "I can't believe she would say that!" "There's no way that is possible." They were overwhelmed with the horror the father must have been experiencing right then. He denied it but said, "Whatever you want me to do, I'll do it." He stepped down from leadership and began the process of trying to repair his family.

We had set up counseling to begin for the family, which they all attended. Except Donna. Her father came to every meeting we scheduled with pastors. She did not. In fact, she disappeared. No one saw her or heard from her again for months. Of course we began to question her trustworthiness. Where was she? It was as if she pulled the pin on a grenade and left town. Why wasn't she walking through all the steps we had predetermined before the confrontation? This was all a mystery. Until almost a year later.

Donna's mother and father and sister were sitting at home one evening when the front door opened. In walked Donna. She stood there in the living room, staring at her stunned family, and uttered these words: "I made it all up. I'm sorry." The admission that it was all made up was not a shock to them. They knew it, and they had been trying to tell all of us that it was a hoax. The apology was a surprise, but the most shocking thing said that night was not the admission or the apology, it was what Donna's father said: "Welcome home."

Mercy.

TO-DO LIST

- If there is anyone you're close to that you are carrying resentment toward, try your best to show mercy or even begin working through the forgiveness process.
- Perhaps there is someone that you have personally wronged and you know it. Go to that person this week and ask for mercy from them while admitting your fault.

DISCUSSION QUESTIONS

1. What is something that you would consider unforgivable? What would it look like for mercy to be applied in those situations?
2. Do you have an example of unfailing love or mercy that has been displayed in your own life?
3. What is the difference between justice and mercy? How can they go together?

ten

For Those We Don't Know and Don't Love

School lunchrooms can be cruel.

While standing in line waiting to get my lunch, I have only one thing on my mind: Where will I sit? It was my first day at this high school, and where to sit in the lunchroom was my chief concern. Sure, I had some friends, but I was not certain they were at this lunch period. What would I do if I had no one? I grabbed my plate and began the slow walk. You don't want to appear to be wandering . . . that's a sure giveaway that you have no place. No table. No friends.

Certain tables were clear on who was allowed, like the athletes' table—mainly football players, some basketball players, and of course the weight lifters. They were often eating meat, and lots of it. The wrestlers were eating nothing because they were "pulling weight" for an upcoming tournament. And all the jocks were wearing sweat suits, hoodies, some tank tops (the greatest fashion mistake in our lifetime), and jerseys. But one thing was clear:

non-athletes need not ask to join. Though I considered myself athletic, I had not yet made it into this club. I kept walking.

Next up was the cool table. These kids wore the best clothes. Threw the best parties. Told the jokes everyone thought were hilarious. And they somehow managed to escape high school with no acne. How did they do it? They would talk about how ridiculous others dressed, how insignificant other tables were, and how great their parents were doing in their businesses. This was the top of the mountain. But it was not my peak to climb. I took my JCPenney clothes and walked right past their Ralph Lauren flair. Don't look and they may not notice you.

Then there were, how shall I say it . . . the nerds. The geeks. The smart kids with glasses and pocket protectors. The kids at this table were smarter than all their teachers, and they knew it and talked openly about it. They would one day have jobs making more than all of us but would probably never move out of their parents' basement. They spent lunch playing Dungeons and Dragons and talking about the latest sci-fi novel. Others were allowed to sit here because when you are at the bottom of the social ladder, you tend to be more welcoming, but don't expect to understand anything they are saying. The only way to pull this off was to act like they were helping you with your homework. I kept walking.

There was a Christian table. This was a collection of kids from local churches who somehow gravitated together to make it through high school with a guaranteed prom date yet accountability to prevent a pregnancy scare. The problem with this table was that it was exclusive and not everyone could join. Plus weird things would randomly happen, like breaking into song and banging cups on the table. Even though I'm a Christian, I kept walking.

Fortunately, there was a catchall table. A lost-and-found of kids. A place for those of us wandering in the abyss of the cafeteria. This table worked for us. We always wanted to be at another table.

We openly mocked the other tables, but we longed to be invited to sit with them.

Over the next few months and my following years of high school, I found my table. A careful selection of students who were just like me. They looked like me. They talked like me. And they thought like me. It's always great to find your table.

We all search for our table.

We like to gather with people who are like us. After the 2016 presidential election, stunning stats revealed how much birds of a feather flock together. Between 1992 and 2016, the share of voters living in politically extreme landslide counties quintupled from 4 percent to 21 percent.[1] What does this mean? It means we are moving to areas where people think like us and, yes, vote like us. We like our table.

The problem is, there are a lot of people who don't fit at our table. And when we are called to "love mercy," that mercy is to extend beyond those like us. Pastor Clay Scroggins goes so far as to state that our view of God is the size of our table. We tend to view God as having the same political, personality, spending, and entertainment preferences as ourselves. The smaller our table, the smaller our God. Probably because our God is a God of inclusion and mercy.

> We tend to view God as having the same political, personality, spending, and entertainment preferences as ourselves. The smaller our table, the smaller our God.

The second way that the word *hesed* is used when it comes to mercy is when there is no reason to be generous or merciful to them, or there is no prior relationship between you and them, but you nevertheless act generously or mercifully by remaining faithful or committed to them. In other words, you give them this gift of mercy even if they cannot repay you, you don't even know them, or they are not at your table.

How Jesus Did This

Jesus modeled this for us. John tells us about one of the trips they took as disciples. They were headed to Jerusalem, and John says that Jesus "had to go through Samaria." No Jew "had" to go through Samaria. In fact, Jews would avoid walking through Samaria at all costs. To Jews, Samaritans were a religious and ethnic hybrid, a result of the inbreeding of Assyrians and Jews after the exile. These people were not pure Jews. This was the impure Jews table, and the disciples were not comfortable with it.

John begins to give us some details of their journey:

> So he came to a town in Samaria called Sychar, near the plot of ground Jacob had given to his son Joseph. Jacob's well was there, and Jesus, tired as he was from the journey, sat down by the well. It was about noon. When a Samaritan woman came to draw water, Jesus said to her, "Will you give me a drink?"
>
> John 4:5–7

As if it wasn't bad enough that Jesus was on Samaritan soil, now he is talking to a Samaritan woman. Men did not socialize with women. They were not welcome at the male table. But that didn't stop Jesus. In fact, whoever says that Christianity is misogynistic and sexist doesn't know Jesus. Jesus extended acceptance beyond gender time and time again. Jesus allowed this woman into the boys' club. She could sit at his table.

But there was another obstacle. Any idea why this woman would come out and draw water from the well at noon, in the heat of the day? It was because she didn't want to be seen by all the other women of the town, who came out early. It might have had something to do with the scarlet letter she wore.

After she and Jesus have conversed for a moment, Jesus makes a very interesting statement to us, but he's digging below the surface with her.

He told her, "Go, call your husband and come back."

John 4:16

Much like an attorney, Jesus never asks a question or makes a statement to which he doesn't know the answer. And the answer is that she does not have a husband. It is at this point we learn the reason she's wanting to be left alone, the reason she draws water in the heat of the day, the reason she says she has no husband. She sits at the relationship-failure table.

Jesus said . . . "The fact is, you have had five husbands, and the man you now have is not your husband."

John 4:18

No one could administer both mercy and truth at the same time like Jesus. As he's underlining her failure, he's restoring her with his attention. He's telling her, "I'm talking to you, I'm accepting you, and yes, I do know your biggest regrets, failures, and secrets. I know you feel alone. Used. A relational failure. But you can sit with me."

Maybe this is why Jesus had to go through Samaria. He wanted to add her to his table.

Author Richard Beck describes this as expanding your moral circle.[2]

Fully human	Infra-human	Not human	Not there
Family Friends "Like Family" KIN Us	Acquaintances Strangers	Those we see as less than human NOT KIN Them	Animals Monsters	[Invisible people]
Ends in themselves	Means to our ends		

139

Our lunch table is filled with our friends and our family. And anyone like family. Those who like us and are like us. Beyond this are the strangers that we meet. We see them. They exist. Yet even though they are still human, as Beck says, they are strangers nonetheless.

Beyond this category are the unseen, unknown masses. The people in other countries, other socioeconomic groups, those we read about and hear about but we don't know their names. We don't know their story. And as a result, they are less than real and even less than human to us. The only time they exist is when they are a means to our end. A group to buy our product or promote our mission, or even people to make us look like we are caring and justice filled. We want to advocate for them, to support them, but we don't know them. Truth be told, we are more interested in you THINKING we know them and care about them than we are in actually knowing them.

A few years ago our church decided to build a student building. Our history at Real Life Church is to tithe off of every dollar we receive for our ministry. And when it comes to capital campaigns, we do the same. Over the years we've built orphanages, feeding centers, and community centers around the world in addition to church facilities on our property. So when this new project came up, we knew we would be doing something for someone else, but who?

> Truth be told, we are more interested in you THINKING we know them and care about them than we are in actually knowing them.

After prayerful consideration, we decided to partner with Stadia and Compassion to build two churches in South America and then sponsor the children in the areas of these churches. What a thing for our church to celebrate and get behind! We were all excited about helping kids in our community and in Bolivia. My preteen daughters decided to sponser a child themselves . . . albeit with a bit of a push from my wife and me. To be honest, I had a lot of pride standing up before our congregation declaring, "This is how much we care about these kids in Bolivia—my daughters are using baby-sitting money to sponsor a little boy named Daniel. Join us!" But even though we had a packet of information complete with pictures of Daniel, he was still not in our circle. He was a photograph. An idea. Someone who received support from an organization we supported on his behalf. But not really at our table.

I don't think I really understood this until I actually went to Bolivia and met Daniel. We took a small video team from our church down to film the progress of the building we were funding and to meet some of the children we had sponsored. I had come equipped with letters and toys from my girls for Daniel and his siblings. But I was not prepared for how I would feel.

I came down from my hotel room to the lobby to find a small welcoming committee of Daniel, his mother, his brother, and a cousin. They were holding a sign that said "Welcome Pastor Rusty George." I was speechless. A bit embarrassed, but humbled at their gratitude. I hugged them, gave them gifts, and with the help of a translator, spoke a few words to Daniel. It was a perfect intro-duction and, to be honest, an ideal photo op. But when I realized we were all boarding a bus and spending the day together, I was overwhelmed. What were my responsibilites with Daniel? What did he expect? What would we talk about? After all . . . he's not at my table. He's not in my circle. He's at the "kids table." He's at the "table that speaks another language." So when we got on the bus, he sat down . . . and I walked to the back of the bus. I rationalized this as *He won't want to hang out with an adult he doesn't even know.* I was wrong.

Daniel and his family called me up to sit with him. Even though Daniel was a picture to me, I was part of his family. He included me in his circle. He invited me to sit at his table. Over the rest of the day we learned to communicate as best we could. I showed him pictures of my kids. We played with the toy cars my kids had sent. He taught me songs they sang in church. And I heard stories about his family from his mother. Nagging me in the back of my mind was that still, small voice that I knew to be the Holy Spirit—"He's not just a sermon illustration. He's real." Extending mercy to Daniel was more than sending in my kids' money. It was sitting on a bus and becoming friends.

I wonder in our age of social justice and social media how many of us fall prey to the temptation to wield someone else's plight as our crusade? Isn't it easy to show impoverished people or the poorly educated and use it as a platform to rail against the government? But do we know these people whose pictures we plaster on our social media sites? We just see them as illustrations. Isn't it easy every time there is a tragedy such as a school shooting to send prayers, sympathy, and silence but also rail against gun control or local officials or the negligent parents in an attempt to leverage our political stance or social position? But we don't know them. We haven't sat with them. We haven't invited them to our table.

> Jesus reminds us that showing mercy is not just for those in our circle, but for those who would never assume they could be part of it.

Jesus reminds us that showing mercy is not just for those in our circle, but for those who would never assume they could be part of it. So Jesus widens the circle.

Who Is Your Samaritan Woman?

For many of us, the person we are least likely to invite to our table may very well be someone of another race, nationality, or heritage.

For some of us it may be a person who is in another socioeconomic category. It's the server at the restaurant. Or it's the people whose house we clean. They are not "one of us."

But some of us are a bit more sophisticated in our prejudice. We use the Bible to back us up. We condemn pastors who teach differently from our preference. We condemn churches that use methods we are not comfortable with. We avoid interactions with non-Christians because "Bad company corrupts good morals." And we even look in judgment at those who are doctrinally different from us.

Pastor Andy Stanley tells of a conversation he was having with his father, Pastor Charles Stanley. They were discussing a book that had recently come out and was creating quite a stir in the Christian community. The author suggested that hell may not be real but is more of a metaphor. After debating the validity of the statement and the disgust at the departure from historical Christianity, Andy looked at his dad and said, "But, Dad . . . don't you hope he's right?"[3] The moment I heard that story I felt a check in my spirit. Do I really want mercy for all . . . or just for me?

For most of us, though, our Samaritan woman is simply whoever makes us uncomfortable. Anyone who will push us out of our comfort zone. Anyone who challenges our thinking. Anyone who pushes our buttons. Anyone whom we see as a waste of our time. All of these people are not welcome at our table.

But what Jesus does is show us the value of pulling up a chair and saying, "Have a seat."

The interaction between Jesus and this woman is so engaging for her that it changes her life. Her first reaction is to say, "You must be a prophet!" Once she knows she's in the presence of greatness, she begins to discuss where to worship. The Jews say one thing, we say another. And Jesus then redefines her definition of worship.

> "A time is coming and has now come when the true worshipers will worship the Father in the Spirit and in truth, for they are the kind of worshipers the Father seeks. God is spirit, and his worshipers must worship in the Spirit and in truth."
>
> John 4:23–24

143

It's not about a place. It's about a person. I am the one you have been waiting for. Pull up a chair.

It might have been Jesus who asked for a drink, but in the end, she received living water. Her reaction is stunning. She runs off and tells all the people she tried to avoid all about Jesus. The one who had received mercy . . . gave mercy. All those who had excluded her and judged her and whispered about her . . . they still needed mercy as much as she did. They still longed for living water. And she offered them a drink.

A Simple Way to Follow

Find that person you often overlook and grant them mercy.

It may be a look. It may be time. It may be conversation. It may be assistance. But it will cost you. And it might take you out of your comfort zone. But it will be worth it. If not for them, certainly for you.

Maybe it's a co-worker who you barely know. Have you considered they are just as human as you? They have hopes and dreams like you. They have a family. They worry about their kids. They struggle to make ends meet. They have regrets. They have memories and stories they'd love for someone to hear. Just like you. Invite them to sit at your table.

Maybe it's a neighbor who you never speak to. You wave once in a while, but you drive straight home and close the garage door behind you. Ever thought about what they talk about in their home? Maybe they argue about money. Maybe they just found drugs in their daughter's room. Maybe they have a son who just got accepted to an Ivy League school. They have stories and dreams and fears . . . just like you. Maybe like Kristin Schell, as she talks about in her book *The Turquoise Table*, you should paint a picnic table turquoise, put it in your front yard, and start inviting your neighbors to sit at your table.[4]

Maybe it's the barista that serves your coffee. Did you know she's a single mom working three jobs just to pay the bills? While you stand there with your three kids on family day, she's longing for a day to spend with hers. And while you see her as a means to an end—getting your order right—she's wondering, if tomorrow will be any better than today.

I don't always know who it is for me. I don't always recognize it. But one day God made it pretty clear. Annoyingly so. I had been saving up to buy a new grill. Not just any grill—the Big Green Egg. The BGE is a ceramic grill that provides the greatest smoked or grilled meats in the history of creation. You can grill on the spot or go low and slow for twenty-four hours. Whatever your culinary preference. The only sticking point is they are expensive. Very expensive. But . . . I had saved up. I'd been visiting a local barbecue supply store in prep for this very day, and I had cash in hand and was headed to collect my bounty. But on the way to the store, something unexpected happened. As I drove past Walmart, I saw a homeless woman standing outside with two young kids and a baby. She was holding a sign asking for help, and I could not look away.

God grabbed my heart that day as if to say, "You're headed to buy an extravagant grill, and she just needs some food. You can get a cheaper grill." It was at this point I began to regret the route I had taken and the store I had chosen to buy my grill. I felt like I was starting to argue with God a bit. I felt I could since Abraham did . . . although he did it in an effort to keep God from raining fire down on a city of people. I was arguing for the right to bring smoke down on a rack of ribs. I'm embarrassed to say how long the arguing lasted. I probably put a few miles on the car circling the parking lot while negotiating with myself. But in the end, God won. And he was right.

I pulled over, got out of my car, and walked up and started talking with this woman. She didn't speak much English but enough to let me know their difficult situation. I reached into my pocket, pulled out a handful of cash, and gave it over to her. She was overwhelmed. She cried. I cried. I left and went home and bought a cheaper grill online. (You might be asking, "Why didn't you give her all the money?" God didn't tell me to. Maybe I dropped the call before he got specific.) Regardless, something happened that day to me.

My circle got a little bigger. My table got a few more chairs.

TO-DO LIST

- Consider making a commitment to look at each person you encounter during the course of the day, and mentally pause to think of them and see them as a person God loves dearly.
- Pray to have the opportunity to extend mercy to someone every morning for a week and see what happens! Try not to argue with God *too much*.

DISCUSSION QUESTIONS

1. Which "table" did you sit at? Was it welcoming or exclusive?
2. In this chapter, Clay Scroggins said that our view of God is the size of our table. How big would you say your table is in your life right now, on a scale of 1 to 10?
3. The moral circle that Richard Beck talks about was mentioned in this chapter as well. Where in our society do you see this kind of exclusion taking place the most? Where do you see people being accepted the most?
4. How do you think the church can get better at this?

eleven

Receiving Mercy

t was my stupid idea. My parents were coming to town and we needed a new mattress. So I found one.

At our church's version of Goodwill.

Sure, I know what you're thinking. Big spender. Nothing but the best for Mom and Dad. But Lorrie and I had only been married for a few years, so the income was tight, and purchasing a new mattress for a few visitors a year seemed irresponsible. So I opted for free. I asked if they had a queen size. And they did. At least it was queen and not twin. I'm not a monster.

I headed down one Saturday afternoon to get the mattress. I didn't have a truck or a flatbed, so I took what I had. A car. My plan was to tie it to the roof. After all, I'd seen this done before. What could possibly go wrong? I rolled into the parking lot of our thrift store like a man with a plan. I had a mattress on reserve and was about to hoist it onto the top of my Saturn sedan like a boss. I even had my own tie-downs. Bungee cords. I was ready.

Someone helped me carry the mattress to the car and helped me plop it on the roof. I said, "I've got it from here." Carefully and thoughtfully I arranged the cords on top and then through the windows. They stretched to their limit, but seemingly not too tight. This was foolproof. I started out in the parking lot driving with caution. Can't be too careful. For added security I put my arm out the window and held on to the mattress to give it some extra support. Because if the bungee cords couldn't withstand the 55 mph headwind, surely my left arm would be able to restrain it. As I got out on the open road, my confidence in my tie-down job turned to hubris. I started driving a bit faster. I needed to get home. But somewhere out in the middle of nowhere, and despite my cords and my bicep, the mattress blew off my car with a force and snap like I'd never seen. Instinctively I glanced in my rearview mirror and saw my mattress bouncing down the two-lane highway. Quickly I hit the brakes and made a rushed U-turn. I pulled over near the mattress, which was now in the ditch, and I had two thoughts—one, how will I get this out of here and back on the car, and two, I can't ever tell my parents how I got their mattress!

Parking on the shoulder, I made my way down into the ditch to retrieve my junkyard find. This was not as easy as when I first put it on the car. As I was struggling to get it out of the ditch and toward my car, another car stopped. Out bounced a middle-aged man with mercy in his eyes. (He looked a lot like Michael Landon.) He came over and offered no judgment. He never said, "What in the world have you done?" or "I've never seen anyone so stupid . . ." but instead, he began to help. He helped me carry it to the car. He helped me place it on the roof. And then he even helped me tie it down in a way that was sure to hold. He never gave advice. He never laughed under his breath. He didn't even take any pictures. (Something I'm not sure I would have resisted.) He just helped. And as kind as this was, something inside me wanted to shout, "It's okay, I've got it!" After all, it was my stupid idea. I should have to live with the consequences. But he didn't let me.

Sometimes the hardest person to offer mercy toward is yourself.

It can be difficult to offer compassionate and faithful mercy to those you do not know. It can be even more difficult to offer it to those you know . . . and who should know better. But sometimes the hardest person to offer mercy toward is yourself.

"You Don't Know What I've Done"

For many of us, mercy is a dish easy to serve others but not ourselves, due to the fact that we know who we are. It's similar to watching people's lives on Facebook and Instagram. We see their highlight reels and we see our blooper reels. We see their perfect smiling pictures and we hear our screaming, angry family. And when it comes to the mercy of God, we see others' minor indiscretions or miraculous conversion experiences and think, *Sure, God loves* you, *forgives* you, *and will use* you. But I know who I am. I know how worthless I feel. My crimes may be silent and small, but they are big to me. And I'm sure they are big to God. God loves you, forgives you, and will use you . . . but not me.

One day I was having lunch with a wonderful man in our church who had been serving faithfully in several areas of ministry. He was successful in business, family, and now ministry, and by all accounts seemed to have the world by a string. But over lunch he began to unpack his life for me. I asked him about how he came to Christ, expecting to hear that he grew up in a Christian home, gave his life to Jesus at church camp, and has an ichthus tattoo on his shoulder and a copy of *Jesus Calling* on his bedside table. But instead he led with this: "For thirty years I was a non-believing successful businessman who did cocaine every day when I came home from work." So much for the ichthus. I was stunned. He went on to tell me that one of the hardest things about his coming to Christ was not forgiving others, was not admitting his own sin, but rather accepting Christ's forgiveness. Even though no one else knew his habit, HE did. And it was hard to believe Christ could forgive what he himself could not.

Maybe for you so far in this book you've been thinking, *I can do this. I can act justly. I can stand up for the oppressed, meet the needs of the poor, and bring dignity to the disgraced. I can even love mercy. I can forgive my brother-in-law. I can offer grace to those who have offended me. I can even let people off the hook.* But the biggest struggle you have is to let yourself off the hook. How can God forgive you when you can't forgive yourself? How can you follow Jesus if it means to show mercy to even yourself?

I know that was the case for Colt.

Colt was eighteen and in high school when his dangerous and reckless living caught up with him. He had grown up far from God, experimenting with drugs and alcohol, and living the teenage dream. So he thought. One afternoon while street racing, his car went out of control and he hit a tree going near 100 mph. When the ambulance arrived, they made two quick assessments: First, Colt may not make it. And second, the passenger in the car, Colt's best friend, was dead.

One of our pastors was Colt's neighbor. When he got the news, he headed to the hospital only to find Colt in a coma with a 10 percent chance of survival and little chance of regaining any normal function. Colt's family was devastated and cried out to God and even against God. Five days later, Colt woke up.

Two weeks later, Colt had regained enough of his motor skills and function that he was discharged. For the next seven months Colt had to relearn how to walk, talk, and swallow. And over that time, Colt faced the overwhelming guilt of being responsible for the death of his best friend. During this time he attempted suicide. How could he live with himself and what he had done? Colt was eventually charged with second-degree homicide for the death of his friend. Even though he had beaten the odds and survived, he was now headed to prison. And emotionally speaking, he was already there. How could he ever forgive himself for what he had done?

Maybe you haven't been in physical prison but you know emotional isolation, you know spiritual depravity. You know what it's like to have guilt so strong that it keeps you up at night, keeps you distant in relationships, and makes forgiveness unacceptable. After all, if they knew what you knew . . . they'd never accept you.

Author and proclaimed shame expert Brené Brown states, "It's always helpful to remember that when perfectionism is driving, shame is riding shotgun." She goes on to say, "Shame hates it when we reach out and tell our story. It hates having words wrapped around it—it can't survive being shared. Shame and secrecy. When we bury our story, the shame metastasizes."[1]

How about for you? Has shame taken over?

Much like justice, mercy can be easier to extend than receive. How can we live in mercy and let mercy lead in our lives without walking in guilt and shame?

Do Micah's words have anything to do with Colt's story, or your story, or mine? And isn't it possible to love God and follow Jesus without having to deal with showing mercy to ourselves?

The author of Hebrews seems to have a take on it.

> And without faith it is impossible to please God, because anyone who comes to him must believe that he exists and that he rewards those who earnestly seek him.
>
> Hebrews 11:6

In what is often referred to as the "Hall of Faith" chapter in the Bible, the author lists name after name of giants in our faith who did great things for God. And they all had one thing in common: faith.

Faith is not the absence of fear. Faith is not the absence of regret. Faith is not the absence of sin. Faith is belief that God is real, and he will reward me when I seek him—regardless of who I am or what I have done.

And this must be the case, because when you read through this list, you find quite a few people who wouldn't be invited to Christmas dinner in most homes.

Noah—got drunk and went streaking

Abraham—a liar who pimped out his wife

Isaac—played favorites with his kids

Jacob—a cheat and a liar

Joseph—arrogant

Moses—a murderer

Rahab—a prostitute

These are the people who did great things for God. Ever think they wrestled with accepting his mercy?

Earlier in the letter to the Hebrews, the author gives us some more detail as to what we can expect when we approach God:

Let us then approach God's throne of grace with confidence, so that we may receive mercy and find grace to help us in our time of need.

Hebrews 4:16

When we approach God, the one who knows everything we've ever done or thought about doing, we can approach with confidence. Confidence in what? His judgment? His anger? His disappointment? No, his mercy and his grace. These are the two things you can absolutely count on from God. Mercy and grace.

Paul had to wrestle with this.

Much like Colt, he knew the pain of his past. But he was somehow able to move on. How could a man who had imprisoned Christians now become one? How could he sit at the church dinners with them now? How could he approach Jesus with confidence when he had worked so hard to end the movement of Jesus?

Paul even tells us what he thinks of himself in 1 Timothy 1:15: "Christ Jesus came into the world to save sinners—of whom I am the worst."

He doesn't say I *was* the worst, but I AM the worst. Forgiven? Yes. But still, I've out-sinned you all!

How could Paul come to the throne of God with such confidence? How could he move beyond his past? How could he go on to do such great things for God when he so adamantly states "I am the worst sinner among us"? He indicates that in a letter to the Corinthians.

> I care very little if I am judged by you or by any human court; indeed, I do not even judge myself. My conscience is clear, but that does not make me innocent. It is the Lord who judges me.
>
> 1 Corinthians 4:3–4

Tim Keller points out

> When he says that he does not let the Corinthians judge him nor will he judge himself, he is saying that he knows about his sins but he does not connect them to himself and his identity. His sins and his identity are not connected. He refuses to play that game. He does not see a sin and let it destroy his sense of identity. He will not make a connection. Neither does he see an accomplishment and congratulate himself. He sees all kinds of sins in himself —and all kinds of accomplishments too—but he refuses to connect them with himself or his identity. So, although he knows himself to be the chief of sinners, that fact is not going to stop him from doing the things that he is called to do.[2]

Paul had reached a point where not only did others' opinions not matter to him, neither did his own.

Keller writes

Every single day, we are on trial. That is the way that everyone's identity works. In the courtroom, you have the prosecution and the defense. And everything we do is providing evidence for the prosecution or evidence for the defense. Some days we feel we are winning the trial and other days we feel we are losing it. But Paul says that he has found the secret. The trial is over for him. He is out of the courtroom. It is gone. It is over. Because the ultimate verdict is in. Now how could that be? Paul puts it very simply. He knows that they cannot justify him. He knows he cannot justify himself. And what does he say? He says that it is the Lord who judges him. It is only His opinion that counts.[3]

How Jesus Did This

While Jesus never needed to extend mercy to himself, he certainly models for us the key trait of this concept—faith in the Father.

We underestimate the level of faith that Jesus displayed because we think, well, of course, he's Jesus. But at what point did he know that? Do we assume that as a baby he was well aware that he had orchestrated the cosmos? He probably knew because Mary and Joseph told him. He had to have faith.

While our walking into our baptism requires faith in the Father's forgiveness, his walking into his baptism required faith in the Father's plan. It was at this moment that he hears from his Father, "This is my son, in whom I am well-pleased."

Immediately he is led out into the desert to pray, fast, and be tempted by the devil. And with each temptation to cut corners and take a shortcut to his mission, he must have faith in the Father that his plan is best.

Each time he prays for the Father to heal someone, to feed someone, or to bring someone back from the dead, he is exhibiting faith in his Father to provide.

And then in the Garden of Gethsemane we see Jesus show his strongest display of faith.

> He fell with his face to the ground and prayed, "My Father, if it is possible, may this cup be taken from me. Yet not as I will, but as you will."
>
> Matthew 26:39

Jesus, though being all-knowing, had limited his knowledge and power to be human. So he had to trust his Father.

A Simple Way to Follow

It is with this same trust and faith that we must believe him when he says we are forgiven. We don't extend mercy to ourselves because we deserve it or even because we think we've earned it. We extend it because the Father has extended it. And we have faith in the Father. Just like Jesus.

In the end, this helps us actually extend mercy and compassion toward others.

> As it turns out, we can't practice compassion with other people if we can't treat ourselves kindly.
>
> Brené Brown[4]

I like what Paul says,

> The law was brought in so that the trespass might increase. But where sin increased, grace increased all the more, so that, just as sin reigned in death, so also grace might reign through righteousness to bring eternal life through Jesus Christ our Lord.
>
> Romans 5:20–21

One Monday morning I was hauling the garbage cans out to the curb for trash pickup later that day. It was a standard process of three cans, each with a separate purpose: one for greens, one for recyclables, and one for all other trash. The only problem was I had more trash than I could fit in the garbage cans. We had purchased some furniture and one of the boxes was too big, so I did what most would do: I consolidated. I took the oversized box and loaded my extra trash bags that wouldn't fit in the garbage can into this box. I felt I was being kind. After all, I could have just piled everything up on the curb and let them deal with it. But instead it was the three garbage cans and one big box with trash inside. Nice and neat. Grace and mercy, so I thought.

> We don't extend mercy to ourselves because we deserve it or even because we think we've earned it. We extend it because the Father has extended it.

When I came home later that day, I discovered that while the garbage cans had been emptied, the big box of trash was still there—with a note. The note read like red marks on a term paper. An act of scolding. It simply read, "Don't hide your trash." Clearly they had not enjoyed my consolidating. And clearly they would not be accepting my big box of trash. Their message could not have been more direct. And the power of that message transcends trash and garbage cans. Don't hide your trash. Get it out. Give it to Jesus. Tell it to others. And accept with confidence the grace and mercy only the Father can provide.

This is what Colt eventually came to accept. It is only Jesus' opinion that counts. Through his neighbor and some other faithful people from the church, he began to hear of God's love and forgiveness for him through Jesus. And he approached the throne of Jesus with confidence. Not in what he himself had done, but in what Jesus had done.

Again, as Brené Brown says

Our job is not to deny the story, but to defy the ending—to rise strong, recognize our story, and rumble with the truth until we get to a place where we think, Yes. This is what happened. And I will choose how the story ends.[5]

Colt is choosing how his story will end. During his time in prison, he studied the Bible and led Bible studies. And after three years, he was released to write a new story for his life. He enrolled in Bible college and is pursuing ministry. He is living each day in grace and mercy.

Each day is our own gift to relish in the grace and mercy of God too. Accepting it, choosing where our own story ends, can be one of the hardest things we ever do, but it will most certainly be the best thing we ever do.

TO-DO LIST

Take ten to twenty minutes and practice a "stillness prayer." Try this for an outline:

- Find a quiet place and sit very still. Become aware of any tension you're carrying from your head down to your toes, and try to relax.
- Now that your body is relaxed, try relaxing your brain. Focus on your breathing and do ten-count breaths if you need to.
- Pick a phrase, or a piece of Scripture, and repeat it to yourself, out loud, for a solid five to ten minutes. This could be the Lord's Prayer or a Bible verse of your choice.
- End with the thought that you are loved and unconditionally accepted by God.

- If you feel compelled, journal your experience and perhaps apply what you learned or observed for the next time you do it.
- Write a story about a turning point in your life when you realized that you were loved and cherished by God.

DISCUSSION QUESTIONS

1. Are you someone who easily accepts compliments or not? Why?
2. How do you react to the notion that God accepts you and shows mercy to you?
3. In the Garden of Gethsemane, before he died, Jesus prayed, "Not my will but yours be done." Where do you struggle to live this prayer in your own life?

Step 4

WALK HUMBLY.

twelve

When Confidence
Becomes Pride

I t was a Sunday afternoon, and our church small group was coming over. We were expecting around ten adults and eight kids, so we had been arranging chairs, providing snacks, and making sure the backyard play equipment was ready to use. Around three o'clock people began to arrive. And with every family who entered, their kids would run to the backyard like a jailbreak. They were thrilled to see their friends, swing and slide, and play some made-up game with a ball and a Frisbee. The adults were equally glad to see each other, just less likely to run and jump and throw things. After everyone seemed to be settled in with adequate refreshments and free-flowing conversation, we were about to begin our discussion.

Every church small group must have a formal "discussion." This is code for "answering every question in the back of the Bible study book." Just as we were about to begin, though, an eight-year-old girl who had come inside with a friend earlier, was walking through the house on her way back out. She took one look out the sliding glass door at all of her friends on the swing set and she began to run. The only problem was she didn't notice that the sliding glass door was not open. It was closed. BOOM! The sound of her running body hitting that door was thunderous. Adults gasped, women ran, and her father glanced. "She's fine." And she was fine. But she was pretty shook up by the shock and embarrassment and had burst into tears.

A few women took her into the bathroom to calm her down and wash her face. While she was still crying, her friend finally caught up to her. "What happened?" she asked. To which an adult responded, "She ran into the glass door thinking it was open." The concerned friend seemed to understand, comforted her friend, and then decided to head on outside. Running. Right into the same closed glass door. BOOM! It was at this point someone suggested we leave the door open. Another sharp individual inquired about our glass cleaner. And now two kids were nursing sore noses and bruised egos.

Granted, they were eight. Just kids. But this method of imitating failure is one most of us are familiar with.

My wife and I bought a cheap desk at a garage sale one time. I say desk, but it was actually a door that someone put legs on. It was perfect for what we needed. Tall, long, and cheap. The only weird thing about it was that one of the legs had been cut in half and then reattached with a screw. I was intrigued, but not enough to ask questions at the time of purchase. Like I said, it was cheap.

We brought it home and I propped open the door and began to drag this thing inside. My wife said, "Can I help?" To which I replied, like most men, "No, I've got it." It turns out lifting the door was not the problem. I just couldn't get it through the door! The legs were too long, or the desk was too tall . . . clearly the desk's fault, not mine. After a bit of struggling, my wife calmly suggested, "Maybe that's why the leg can come off? Maybe someone else couldn't get it in the door, so they sawed it off then reattached it." "Maybe," I said audibly. Internally I was thinking, *That's crazy talk. Leave the heavy lifting to me.* This went on for about thirty more minutes. And after I had banged up the walls and bloodied all my knuckles, and just before I was about to take a sledgehammer to the doorframe, I paused and thought, *Maybe she's right.* So when she wasn't looking, I unscrewed the leg, and the desk practically danced into the house. I'll admit, I tried to get the leg reassembled before she discovered what I had done. But I got caught. Bloody knuckles and bruised ego.

Why do I do such things? Clearly someone else had made the same mistake. Clearly my wife had figured it out. But not me. I insisted I had a better way. I could figure this out.

Is it any wonder that the last thing Micah tells everyone, after *act justly and love mercy*, is *walk humbly*? He must know our nature to go at it alone and learn from no one. He must know that if we are just, we'll want everyone to know it. And if we are merciful, we'll post and tweet it for the world to see. So with one last bit of direction, he says to do all of this "humbly . . . with your God."

Granted, knowing our God can make humility easier. And grasping humility will make justice and mercy easier. But humility is one of the most difficult things to achieve. Once you get it, it seems you lose it. So how do we walk in it? And what does it mean to walk humbly? Are we still able to have confidence?

Jesus tells the story of a dad and his two sons in what has become known as the Parable of the Prodigal Son. In this story the younger brother decides he'd like his inheritance so he can enjoy his youth. In that culture, saying this to your father would be like saying, "I wish you were dead so I could get the life insurance." In Jesus' story, the man liquidates his assets and gives the money to his son to do as he pleases. He takes the money and heads to Vegas for a few months, blows it all and ends up slopping the hogs. He comes home hoping to at least be allowed to live with his father's servants, and instead his dad throws a party for him. Everyone attends except the older brother, who stays outside and pouts. When Dad goes out to console him, he finds the older brother is bitter because "Dad never threw a party for *me*!"

In this epic story rich with meaning, we mine out this one of many principles: Only the humble can enjoy the party! The wayward son humbles himself and heads home. The older son stiffens his neck and marches outside. Some of Jesus' audience may have assumed this older son was faithful, dedicated, hardworking, and confident. But Jesus reminds us that he was also arrogant. While the younger brother may have been foolish and reckless, he had sense enough to know when to humble himself and come home. Not so much for the older brother.

Arrogance seems to be the tipping point for every epic story of failure.

In the Old Testament we read the story of the Tower of Babel. These people had become so confident in their abilities that they decided to build a tower to the heavens—so high and big that we would "make a name for ourselves" (Genesis 11:4). This confidence slipped into arrogance and God scattered them.

Greek mythology gives us the story of Icarus, Son of Daedalus, who dared to fly on wings of feathers and wax. He ignored his father's instructions not to fly too close to the sun. When the wax in his wings melted, he tumbled out of the sky and fell into the sea, where he drowned.

Babylonian history tells us of King Nebuchadnezzar, who ruled from 620 BC to 539 BC. Despite his taking captive of the Hebrew youth, he comes to profess Yahweh as God twice: once after Shadrach, Meshach, and Abednego survive a fiery furnace, and another after Daniel interprets his dream. Yet despite his confession and the clear evidence of God in his life, he slips back into arrogance by taking credit for all his success.

As the king was walking on the roof of the royal palace of Babylon, he said, "Is not this the great Babylon I have built as the royal residence, by my mighty power and for the glory of my majesty?"

Daniel 4:29–30

That seems to be the last straw for God for he speaks to Nebuchadnezzar:

"This is what is decreed for you, King Nebuchadnezzar: Your royal authority has been taken from you. You will be driven away from people and will live with the wild animals; you will eat grass like the ox."

Daniel 4:31–32

This lasts for several years and finally a penitent Nebuchadnezzar utters these words: "Those who walk in pride he is able to humble" (v. 37).

Bestselling author and social scientist Jim Collins reflects on the great companies that failed during the Great Recession in his book *How the Mighty Fall*. Collins walks through the five stages of decline. And with no surprise, pride or "hubris born of success" starts it off:

Stage one kicks in when people become arrogant, regarding success virtually as an entitlement, and they lose sight of the true underlying factors that created success in the first place.[1]

This pride then leads to the undisciplined pursuit of more, which leads to a denial of risk and peril, to a fall into grasping for salvation, then into the death spiral.

Walk This Way

Oftentimes in Scripture, "walking" is a metaphor for life. Kings of old were commanded to "walk" in the ways of Torah. Jesus gives his hearers two examples of life, one walking through the wide gate and one walking through the narrow way (Matthew 7:13–14). Paul admonishes his readers to "keep in step with the Spirit" (Galatians 5:25) and walk in the ways of Jesus. So when Micah tells Israel to walk humbly, they would probably have a good idea of what he means.

Oddly enough, the word *humble* isn't used very much in the Old Testament at all. The only other time it is used is in the famous Proverb "When pride comes, then comes disgrace, but with humility comes wisdom" (Proverbs 11:2).

So walking humbly is the opposite of walking pridefully or arrogantly. We use terms like *strutting* or *in your face*, or even *too cool for school* (maybe that was just in my day). Not only is someone who acts this way out of place, to onlookers they can appear laughable.

> **Walking humbly recognizes that you don't own the path you're walking; your very life is a journey with other people.**

Walking humbly is the opposite of that. Walking humbly removes you from center stage and places you in the audience. Walking humbly recognizes that you don't own the path you're walking; your very life is a journey with other people. Walking humbly is walking the narrow road that Jesus was talking about. God requires us to walk hand in hand with one another, and when we do this, we're acting justly and loving mercy while walking humbly with God.

What Micah Said

Now, this is astounding, even for Micah. In Micah 4:5, he mentions walking in the name of God, but walking *with* God? That is something else entirely. He seems to be telling us that when we act justly and love mercy, then we're walking hand in hand with God. God is now our fellow traveler on the road of life. The proud and arrogant don't get that luxury. They're too busy flaunting their money, bragging about their car or house, name-dropping, or reminding us how much they travel and the five-star hotels they stay in. If we're truly walking humbly with God, we're using our lives to enhance the lives of everyone around us. We're demonstrating the self-giving love of Jesus.

The last word to pay attention to here is *tsana*, or "humbly." Unlike the previous two verbs in the phrase that are used abundantly throughout the Old Testament, this one is used only here, which means that something new is going on. It does have a related adjective that comes once in a comment about the "humble" person and the arrogant person referred to in Proverbs 11:2. This may give us a clue as to what Micah is saying.

> Being humble is the opposite of being arrogant.

In other words, being humble is the opposite of being arrogant. People who ignore what God says are in the arrogant category, and the prophets have a lot to say about them. However, I suppose, we can all be arrogant, and that's what makes Micah's three commands here so penetrating.

C.S. Lewis made this revealing observation about pride:

> Pride gets no pleasure out of having something, only out of having more of it than the next person. We say that people are proud of being rich, or clever, or good-looking, but they are not. They are proud of being richer, or cleverer, or better-looking than others. If everyone else became equally rich, or clever, or good-looking there would be nothing to be proud about.[2]

Paul cautions us against this type of pride as he writes to the Corinthians when he uses the words *"puffed up"* (1 Corinthians 4:6). Such an interesting term. Tim Keller points out that this term is rather unique. In fact, this is not the normal hubris word for pride, but rather one that is only used by Paul in the entire Bible.

This term "puffed up" or *physioō*, is a special theme used to correlate the ego with the human body.

> This word used here for pride literally means to be overinflated, swollen, distended beyond its proper size. It is related to the word for 'bellows'. It is very evocative. It brings to mind a rather painful image of an organ in the human body, an organ that is distended because so much air has been pumped into it. So much air, that it is overinflated and ready to burst. It is swollen, inflamed and extended past its proper size. And that, says Paul, is the condition of the natural human ego.[3]

Yet despite all of our warnings about arrogance, pride, and hubris, the apostle Paul encourages us to also be confident, to remain engaged in the battle, and to move ahead with determination.

> I can do all this through him who gives me strength. (Philippians 4:13)

> For God has not given us a spirit of timidity, but of power and love and discipline. (2 Timothy 1:7 NASB)

> We are more than conquerors through him who loved us. (Romans 8:37)

So when does confidence slip into arrogance? And if being a world-changing Christ-follower requires us to walk humbly, how do we possess the confidence required to lead others to Jesus, but the humility required to follow Jesus?

How Jesus Did This

If there was anyone who modeled what it meant to walk in confident humility, it was Jesus. As we discussed before, take another look at how Paul describes him.

In your relationships with one another, have the same mindset as Christ Jesus: Who, being in very nature God, did not consider equality with God something to be used to his own advantage; rather he made himself nothing by taking the very nature of a servant, being made in human likeness. And being found in appearance as a man, he humbled himself by becoming obedient to death—even death on a cross!

Philippians 2:5–8

Despite being God in the flesh, he lived as a man. He had the confidence of being King but the heart of a servant. This is the embodiment of what Brené Brown refers to as the way to live in community: "Have a strong back but a soft front."

Yet none of us would say that Jesus was not confident. This is the same Jesus who turned over the tables outside the temple, is the same Jesus who asked his Father for "another way" to save the world. The same Jesus who powerfully walked through an angry mob ready to throw him off a cliff, leaving all falling on their faces around him. The same Jesus who wept at the tomb of Lazarus.

We see this lived out in the life of Jesus when he is tempted by Satan. He is offered the praises of men and the kingdoms of this world all for the small price of bowing to his tempter. But Jesus will have no part of it. The ends do not justify the means. He remains confident in the battle but humble to his Father.

There is a parable that Jesus tells that I think drives this point home well. In Luke 18:9–14, Jesus tells the parable of the Pharisee and the tax collector. In fact, Luke says he tells this parable specifically "to some who were confident of their own righteousness and looked down on everyone else" (Luke 18:9). Basically, he says, there is a Pharisee and a tax collector, both of whom go to the temple to pray and worship. The Pharisee did all the right things, but it says he thanked God that he was "not like those other people." On the other hand, the tax collector is on his knees, crying to God and beating his chest, begging for forgiveness.

It's pretty easy to hear that parable and immediately apply it to someone else. The irony is, when that is our immediate response, it also automatically makes us the audience. As followers of Jesus we are instructed to be humble, not to look down on others, and to stop categorizing people on a spiritual spectrum. Easier said than done, right? How do we get past this? How can we remain humble and not overly confident?

A Simple Way to Follow

Tim Keller suggests that the way we can follow Jesus in this act of humility, yet also remain confident, is to simply stop connecting every experience, every conversation, with ourselves.

> In fact, I stop thinking about myself. The freedom of self-forgetfulness. The blessed rest that only self-forgetfulness brings. True gospel-humility means an ego that is not puffed up but filled up. This is totally unique. Are we talking about high self-esteem? No. So is it low self-esteem? Certainly not. It is not about self-esteem . . . The truly gospel-humble person is a self-forgetful person whose ego is just like his or her toes. It just works. It does not draw attention to itself. The toes just work; the ego just works. Neither draws attention to itself.[4]

Maybe the first thing we need to do is remind ourselves that it is not about us. This is so counterintuitive because every waking moment is focused on seeking our own comfort or gain: "What do I want to do?" "How can I be happier?" "Where should I go to lunch?" "What's in it for me?" And the moment someone challenges this, we rise up and declare our confident spirit of unalienable rights. "I have a right to McDonalds today!" Perhaps the first thing we do is recognize, It's not about me.

But if that's all we do, we will become reliant on self-talk and self-flagellation to somehow stop thinking of ourselves. We need to put the focus where Jesus did. On the One he walked with and we walk with as well . . . the Father.

Several years ago I was invited by a friend to go fly-fishing in Montana. Normally I'd pass on this since I don't particularly care for fishing. But this was fly-fishing in Montana. And my thoughts immediately envisioned me looking like Brad Pitt in *A River Runs Through It*. (This would not be the last time I'd be compared to Brad Pitt.) It sounded fun and would certainly be a first for me, so I said yes. When I got to the river, I was equipped with waders and a rod and reel, and was encouraged to give it a try. Let me just say, Brad Pitt made it look easier than it actually is! Fortunately they put us in boats with guides. These guides were locals and knew the river like the back of their hand. They had been fly-fishing longer than I had been alive. We were in good hands.

> The first thing we need to do is remind ourselves that it is not about us.

So I, one other rookie, and the guide loaded up in the boat and headed downstream. The guide took us right to where we needed to go. He even put the fly on my line, and told me where to cast. This went on for hours. Casting, mending, reattaching the bait, trying again. It was clear that I would not be in *A River Runs Through It 2*. Finally, after hours of trying, I caught one. And it was awesome. I reeled that fish in like my family depended on it. And even though it was roughly the size of a goldfish, I held it up and took pictures for my kids. This was my moment. It was at this point I looked at our guide and told him he was no longer needed. He could get out at the bank and I'd take it from there. I'd mastered the art of fly-fishing! . . . Of course I hadn't! That would be ridiculous.

I think this is where humility and confidence meet. The humility comes in knowing who I am. The confidence comes in knowing whose boat I'm in.

As we walk through life trying to act justly and love mercy, we don't go alone. We go with our guide, and he knows the waters well.

TO-DO LIST

- Make a list of the areas of your life where you hate to give others credit.
- Write five positive notes or posts about other people's talents.
- Make a practice of celebrating others' happiness.

DISCUSSION QUESTIONS

1. Where would you draw the line between self-confidence and arrogance? Explain.
2. Just like walking in real life, we have to have a good posture, spiritually speaking, if we want to learn to "walk humbly with God." How would you describe your current "posture" toward God?
3. Based on Micah's and Jesus' teachings, how do you think your posture can continue to improve?

thirteen

When Self-Deprecation Becomes a Sin

Who do you think of when I say *pride*?
A politician drunk with power?
An athlete consumed with dominance?
A movie star possessed by fame?

Sure.

How about the donkey from *Winnie the Pooh*—Eeyore?

I didn't think so.

Typically when we think of arrogant, proud, boastful people, we tend to think of the brash, outspoken individual who is always talking about themselves.

Kanye West saying, "I am God's vessel. But my greatest pain in life is that I will never be able to see myself perform live."

Muhammed Ali saying, "I am the greatest!"

Anyone who begins a sentence with "I don't mean to brag, but . . ." A little secret . . . they do mean to brag.

But we don't think of the self-deprecating, low-esteemed, pessimistic cartoon character Eeyore. "Don't worry about me. Go enjoy yourself. I'll just stay here and be miserable." Despite his lack of self-esteem, Eeyore is rather self-obsessed.

Everything is based on how he feels about it. Someone says, "Good morning," he'd say, "If you say so." While he appears to be humble, looks can be deceiving.

Humility is hard to spot and harder to achieve. But let's start with what humility is NOT.

Self-Deprecation

When we talk of walking humbly with our God, the reflex is to lean toward self-deprecation. I am nothing. I am worthless. After all, he is worthy. He is holy. We are not.

So the assumption is that I just need to emphasize my weaknesses, joke about my insecurities, and highlight my faults. But just because I talk down about myself doesn't mean I stop thinking about myself. Often it can be just the opposite.

> When I'm obsessed with my nothingness, my shortcomings, or my inadequacies, I'm still just as obsessed with myself.

When I teach, I use a lot of self-deprecating humor. I have no problem telling you how I lost a mattress off my car roof or had trouble installing a ceiling fan, but teaching it live, I find it sad how I quickly evaluate my worth based on the level of laughter. Did they like me? Do they think I'm funny? What can appear to be "not taking myself too seriously" can often be taken very seriously. My perception of lack of pride becomes my pride.

The flip side of arrogance is self-deprecation. Two sides to the same pride coin. When I'm obsessed with my nothingness, my shortcomings, or my inadequacies, I'm still just as obsessed with myself as Kanye is with himself.

Quiet

It's funny how we are quick to assume that quiet people are humble. In reality, we don't know what is going through their minds as they sit silently. They could be quietly thinking how stupid we all are and how they shouldn't waste their breath on us.

I once knew a very talented musician who led his church in worship every weekend, and to the onlooker it appeared this leader was incredibly humble. He sang and encouraged from stage but was quiet all the rest of the time. Everyone assumed his silence off stage was due to his being in deep communion with the Lord, and when on stage we were witnessing their relationship in action. So when this worship leader left the church for another one, we all assumed the church would now take a dive. After all, the spiritual divining rod had moved. But when this worship leader left, the church didn't tank as many assumed—it took off. I asked a seasoned pastor what he thought the reason was, and his answer was simple: "Pride has left the building." I was a bit stunned and asked what he meant. "He was arrogant. Just because you're quiet doesn't mean you can't think highly of yourself. And now that pride has left, the Holy Spirit has room to work again."

Encouraging

There are some phrases in the church that quickly become associated with spiritual depth. For instance:

"Lord willing, I'll see you next week." That means, "I plan on being here next week, but it's up to God."

"We pray a hedge of protection around you and for Satan to be bound." That means, "I pray that your plans are successful."

"Travel mercies for you." Translation: "I hope you get there safely."

Seemingly humble people have their same expressions:

"It was a team effort." This is what humble people say when they are given credit for doing a good job. They deflect to the team.

"God gets all the glory." Another phrase used often when someone says, "Great job." You can hear this everywhere from the church lobby to the Grammys.

"Bless your heart." This seems genuine and kind, but everyone from the South knows it just means "You're an idiot."

People who say kind, encouraging, positive words to others often appear to be humble. And they may be. But walking in humility is not just becoming an encouraging person. Encouraging seems to be a result of being humble at heart, more than just a pathway toward it.

As mentioned in the last chapter, Micah's goal for us was to walk with God in such a way that we are in awe of who he is. The focus is all on God, not on our arrogance or our deprecation.

And to go along with what was recorded in Proverbs, the result of our humility is wisdom. Often wisdom does not come from just adding deprecation, shyness, or encouragement to our repertoire.

How John Did This

Typically we look at how Jesus did this so we can understand how to follow him. But in this case, let's look at his cousin—John, the baptizer, aka John the Baptist.

John was born before Jesus and was said to be the forerunner or predecessor to clear the way for Jesus. Judging by his adult behavior of living as a recluse in the wilderness, eating locusts and honey, we can only assume he was an interesting child. Growing up hearing how your cousin is better than you might do that to a person. I can imagine all the children eating peanut butter and jelly while John is out back eating bugs off the tree. Preaching to anyone who would listen. Sizing up the family dog for a possible outfit. It came as no shock to his parents when he decided to pack up his sandwich board and head out to the Wild West.

This was a guy who was comfortable with people thinking less of him. He was at ease with people calling him crazy. Yet, is that humility? Confidence in your insanity isn't necessarily a virtue.

But John seems to have something figured out when it comes to his proper place with Jesus.

> Now this was John's testimony when the Jewish leaders in Jerusalem sent priests and Levites to ask him who he was. He did not fail to confess, but confessed freely, "I am not the Messiah." They asked him, "Then who are you? Are you Elijah?" He said, "I am not." "Are you the Prophet?" He answered, "No."
>
> John 1:19–21

John is pretty adamant about who he is not. He refuses to accept any title that is not his. He is not the Messiah, he is not even a prophet. But no self-deprecation, because he does know who he is.

> Finally they said, "Who are you? Give us an answer to take back to those who sent us. What do you say about yourself?" John replied in the words of Isaiah the prophet, "I am the voice of one calling in the wilderness, 'Make straight the way for the Lord.'" Now the Pharisees who had been sent questioned him, "Why then do you baptize if you are not the Messiah, nor Elijah, nor the Prophet?" "I baptize with water," John replied, "but among you stands one you do not know. He is the one who comes after me, the straps of whose sandals I am not worthy to untie."
>
> John 1:22–27

I know exactly who I am. I know my place. I know my role. And I am simply to announce his arrival.

There is something that is freeing about knowing who you are and who you are not. I remember when I first began to learn about spiritual giftedness. Up until that point I felt that as a Christian I was to possess all of the gifts. I needed to be able to teach, lead, administrate, counsel, encourage, give, be merciful, sing, create, and offer hospitality. Just for starters. But when I took a spiritual-gifts test and landed on my top two gifts, it became rather freeing that while I was not off the hook for merciful hospitality, it was not my natural role. My place was to teach and lead.

It must be the way a pitcher in baseball would feel about his batting skills. Greg Maddux is one of the greatest pitchers of all time. But his batting average was a dismal .171. But no one ever said, "If Greg would just work on his batting, he could be something someday." In fact, he didn't even have the greatest arm. Greg Maddux never "lit up the gun," but he knew exactly what pitch to throw and where to place it, and it drove hitters nuts. None of his coaches ever said, "Throw it over 95 miles per hour, and THEN you'll REALLY be something." He already WAS something—a Hall of Fame pitcher! Similar to this, knowing who we are in Christ and for Christ helps us understand how we walk in humility. As John said, "I am simply the voice . . ."

His resolve is so strong that he is even content to lose fans and followers.

> The next day John was there again with two of his disciples. When he saw Jesus passing by, he said, "Look, the Lamb of God!" When the two disciples heard him say this, they followed Jesus.
>
> John 1:35–37

It's at this point in John's life that he has prepared for Jesus, baptized Jesus, and now keeps pointing people to Jesus. And each time he does, his crowd gets smaller. Fewer people follow him as they leave to follow Jesus. And he is fine with that. Humility is like that. Notice John does not say, "I'm a fool. Follow him." He just says, "There he is—the one I exist to serve." And when others go to follow him, it not only fulfills Jesus' call, it fulfills John's mission. Everyone wins when we are humble.

John emphasizes this when someone comes to him and breaks this news to him.

> They came to John and said to him, "Rabbi, that man who was with you on the other side of the Jordan—the one you testified about—look, he is baptizing, and everyone is going to him."
>
> John 3:26

This would be the same as someone saying to you that everyone is leaving your restaurant and going down the street. Or, in my case, everyone is leaving your church and going down the street. Isn't there something in you that says "Wait a minute!" I know there is in me. Not John.

> To this John replied, "A person can receive only what is given them from heaven. You yourselves can testify that I said, 'I am not the Messiah but am sent ahead of him.'"
>
> John 3:27–28

This was not my crowd to begin with. They always belonged to him.

John 3:29 says the bride belongs to the bridegroom. The friend who attends the bridegroom waits and listens for him, and is full of joy when he hears the bridegroom's voice. That joy is mine, and it is now complete.

How do you know when you are humble? It's not when you are quiet or self-deprecating; it's when you are joyful that others get credit. Especially God.

And then John says something that puts all of this in perspective and yet is often misunderstood:

He must become greater; I must become less.

John 3:30

The emphasis here is that Jesus is already great but must be lifted up. Exalted. Made famous. None of us would argue with this. All of John's ministry will be spent to make this happen. He prepared the way for him, he baptized him upon Jesus' direction, and then he kept telling people to look at him . . . the Lamb of God who takes away the sin of the world. He must become greater.

The next line is the one we miss. John doesn't say, "I must become nothing." Or, "I am nothing." But instead, "I must become less." Semantics, you say? Not necessarily. John is leaving room for him to still be something. He's not nothing. He just knows who he is in comparison to Jesus. This is why self-deprecation is not always humility, nor even always needed, because in the kingdom of Jesus the poor are rich, the meek are strong, and the persecuted are lifted up. There is still a place for us to use our gifts, play our part, and be who God has called us to be. The humility comes in knowing our role.

John will eventually have a crisis of faith. Due to John's speaking out against King Herod, he is arrested. Sitting alone in a prison cell will give you time to question your place and purpose . . . and even your faith. And John is not immune to this. Despite his humble acceptance of his role in God's plan, he begins to question the intention of God's plan. Why is he in jail? Why hasn't Jesus rescued him yet? And what if he was wrong all along? What if Jesus isn't the Messiah, but John was confused or made an impulsive decision after a late night or a bad burrito? So John sends word to Jesus: Are you who you say you are? Just give me some assurance.

. . . (John) sent his disciples to ask him, "Are you the one who is to come, or should we expect someone else?"

Matthew 11:2–3

Jesus' reply is direct.

"Go back and report to John what you hear and see: The blind receive sight, the lame walk, those who have leprosy are cleansed, the deaf hear, the dead are raised, and the good news is proclaimed to the poor."

Matthew 11:4–5

We often miss the grace extended in this response. Typically, Jesus would reply with a question or a story, but in this case, knowing John's predicament, he gives him just the facts: blind see, lame walk, leprosy cleansed, deaf hear, dead raised, good news to the poor. John, you got it right. You played your part. Your life was well-lived.

Author Samuel Chand often defines humility as beyond "the space between the temptations of praise and the ravages of blame."[1] John the Baptist finds this space. He doesn't take credit, yet he doesn't blame himself for getting it wrong, let alone deserving of prison for declaring the truth. He has found a way to walk humbly with his Lord.

Timothy Keller writes,

C. S. Lewis in *Mere Christianity* makes a brilliant observation about gospel-humility. If we were to meet a truly humble person they would not be always telling us they were a nobody (because a person who keeps saying they are a nobody is actually a self-obsessed person). The thing we would remember from meeting a truly gospel-humble person is how much they seemed to be totally interested in us. Because the essence of gospel-humility is not thinking more of myself or thinking less of myself, it is thinking of myself less.[2]

A Simple Way to Follow

I know who I am, I know whose I am.

The apostle Paul states in his first letter to the Corinthians that he does not care what others think of him, whether high or low.

> I care very little if I am judged by you or by any human court; indeed, I do not even judge myself.
>
> 1 Corinthians 4:3

Paul is saying that he has reached the place where he is not thinking about himself anymore. When he does something wrong or something good, he does not connect it to himself anymore. His life is all about who he follows.

But he is also aware of who he is called to be and what he has experienced as a result of this. In another letter to the Corinthians, he tackles the criticism he has received regarding possibly not being an authentic disciple. Here is how he responds.

> Are they servants of Christ? (I am out of my mind to talk like this.) I am more. I have worked much harder, been in prison more frequently, been flogged more severely, and been exposed to death again and again. Five times I received from the Jews the forty lashes minus one. Three times I was beaten with rods, once I was pelted with stones, three times I was shipwrecked, I spent a night and a day in the open sea, I have been constantly on the move. I have been in danger from rivers, in danger from bandits, in danger from my fellow Jews, in danger from Gentiles; in danger in the city, in danger in the country, in danger at sea; and in danger from false believers. I have labored and toiled and have often gone without sleep; I have known hunger and thirst and have often gone without food; I have been cold and naked. Besides everything else, I face daily the pressure of my concern for all the churches.
>
> 2 Corinthians 11:23–28

Perhaps the best way for us to understand this is in how Paul sums up this entire passage on boasting and weakness, pride and humility:

> If I must boast, I will boast of the things that show my weakness.
>
> 2 Corinthians 11:30

If needed . . . I'll read you my résumé. If needed . . . I'll list my faults. But everything is for the cause of the One I follow, Christ Jesus. I know my part.

Paul seems to know what to be confident in. And it has everything to do with playing his part for Christ. I know who I am, I know whose I am.

One of the most humble people I know is a pastor by the name of Mike Breaux. Mike has been in ministry for over thirty years and has a deep grounding in who he is in Christ. Years ago, when Mike was first starting out in ministry, he pursued the jet-setting lifestyle of speaking at conference after conference, making a name for himself. But one day God got his attention and seemed to say, "Yes, I gave you a gift to speak, but you are using it to tell others how to take care of their family while you are neglecting yours." So Mike went home. And Mike invested in his kids and his wife. And from that moment, God's call on his life became very clear. His voice seemed to get louder. So much so that when God told him to move to Las Vegas and plant a church, he went.

In Vegas, Mike witnessed thousands come to faith in Christ, many of whom credited Mike. . . . And he would simply thank them, but then redirect them by asking what God had done in their life. In fact, he was so confident in who he was in Christ that when he sensed God call him to leave this young, vibrant, thriving church he started in Vegas and move to a forty-year-old traditional church in Kentucky, he went. No tripping over his ego. No being tied to what he had built, but rather, "I know who I am, and I'll go where he wants me to go."

He announced his decision to leave on the day they launched a capital campaign to build a building. People were mad. Staff threatened to leave. Onlookers thought he was crazy and the church would never survive, but he wasn't tied to their thoughts or opinions. He knew who he was, and whose he was. So he left. When he arrived in Kentucky he inherited a church steeped in tradition but poised for a great impact. And while traditional wisdom says go slow and change nothing for at least a year, he knew God had led him there to make an impact. So he changed everything in one week. As a result, thousands of people came to Christ, and the church exploded with growth. And while people would come to him and say, "You changed my life" or "You got me here," he would respond with, "Thank you. But tell me what God is doing in your life." He accepted who he was but always redirected to the One whom he was following.

Years ago, Brennan Manning told of a priest from Detroit named Edward Farrell who visited his uncle in Ireland in honor of his eightieth birthday. On his uncle's big day, they got up before dawn and walked quietly along the shores of Lake Killarney, then paused to take in the sunrise. They stood there together basking in the beauty of the rising sun when suddenly the uncle turned and went skipping down the road, beaming and smiling from ear to ear. The nephew said, "Uncle Seamus, you really look happy." "I am, lad." "Want to tell me why?" His eighty-year-old uncle replied, "Yes, you see, my Abba is very fond of me."

I know who I am. And whose I am.

TO-DO LIST

- Take a spiritual-gifts assessment.
- List all the ways God uses you on a daily basis.
- Practice saying just "Thank you" when people compliment you.

DISCUSSION QUESTIONS

1. Where would you draw the line between humility and self-deprecation? Explain.

2. In what way do you talk down about yourself?

3. What is it God has created you to do?

fourteen

Giving God His Job Back

Every weekend at our church we do five services. The first one begins on Thursday night, there are three on Sunday morning, and there's a final one Sunday evening. Needless to say, by the time Sunday night rolls around I am tired. Apparently I am not the only one.

One week I was speaking at our last service, 5:00 p.m. Sunday, and midway through my message I began to hear a strange noise from the audience. It was a sound I had heard before, although not in this context. It was the sound of someone snoring. Yep, apparently my talking had put this person to sleep. I thought, *Just keep going, no one will notice*. They did. In fact, a slow rumble of laughter began to roll across the auditorium. I wasn't able to see who was asleep, but I could tell we were all aware someone was. Finally, I broke stride and just started laughing as well. I looked at the audience and said, "Never in my life has there been such evidence that I am doing a horrible job." The laughter erupted, and I'm sure woke this person up. Randomly, for the rest of my message, I would clap just to make sure everyone was awake. While I never found out who it was, anyone who was there will never forget it.

Micah must have felt the same way. Minus the laughter. He and Isaiah and several other prophets would declare and demonstrate, preach and prophesy, and all to no avail. The people did not listen.

They didn't act justly. They didn't love mercy. They didn't walk humbly. And as a result they lived in exile and oppression for the next five hundred years until Jesus came on the scene and said, "This is what I meant." Micah's words fell on deaf ears, but it doesn't have to for us.

In fact, the ability to live out what Micah said is empowered by this last word: *humility*. Humility is clearly defining the roles between you, God, and others. Once you begin to clearly define who does what, humility becomes possible. This allows us to not try to know everything, try to be everywhere, or try to do everything.

Trying to Know Everything

The age of the internet has given all of us a case of FOMO (Fear Of Missing Out). We feel the need to be up to speed on all current events, fashion, business, entertainment, and life hacks. At all times. When our kids ask for help, we pressure ourselves to be able to answer everything. When our co-workers want to brainstorm, we feel the pressure to be right all the time. All of us run the risk of being defensive about any answer we give, because we must be right. All the time.

There's a big word for this: *omniscience*. And it's a word only reserved for God.

Omniscience refers to the description of God as "all-knowing." God knows the past, present, and future. Now, there is some debate on *how* God knows these things, or in what way God knows these things. For instance, many debate on whether God knows what we'll choose tomorrow or simply all the possibilities of what we'll choose tomorrow, and so on and so forth. But the gist is, God knows a lot more than we do and in a way we cannot understand. We see different descriptions of this characteristic of God in places like the Psalms where David describes God as penetrating his thoughts:

You, God, know my folly; my guilt is not hidden from you.

Psalm 69:5

Or places like 1 John 3:20,

For God is greater than our heart and knows all things. (NASB)

The question we have to wrestle with is will we continue to try and know everything, or just trust the One who does?

Trying to Be Everywhere

How many times have we planned our schedule by saying "Yes" and then deciding "How" without ever asking "Should we?" Often when people invite us to do things or ask us to lead projects, our first set of qualifiers are, "Who else will be there?" "What happens if I don't go?" "What if they don't ask again?" Instead of, "Should I go?" This leads many of us to being overscheduled and having little to no margin in our calendars. As a result, we are exhausted and spent. We know we can't physically be everywhere. But we sure try. And even if we can't physically be there, we try to participate in other ways. Ever been that person on a conference call while trying to order at a drive-through while carpooling your kids to a soccer game?

Multitasking is our version of another big word: omnipresence. And it's a description only God can claim.

Omnipresence is the word used to say that God is "all-present." God is everywhere and is boundless, not limited by physicality or

189

mortality, and can be present in all places and in all things. Again, we see this being expressed in the Psalms rather poetically:

Where can I go from your Spirit? Where can I flee from your presence? If I go up to the heavens, you are there; if I make my bed in the depths, you are there. If I rise on the wings of the dawn, if I settle on the far side of the sea, even there your hand will guide me, your right hand will hold me fast.

Psalm 139:7–10

Or as Paul says in Colossians 1:17, "He is before all things, and in him all things hold together." And when Paul quotes the Greek poets while teaching in Athens, "For in him we live and move and have our being" (Acts 17:28).

Do we feel our identity is based on the ability to say YES to every request, or are we humble enough to let God be the only one omnipresent?

Trying to Do Everything

Closely related to trying to be everywhere and know everything is our desire to do everything. We like to not only be the one who has answers for everything, we like to be the person who can fix everything. Nothing a good YouTube video can't fix, right?

When my kids were young they would bring me their toys for repairs. This was easy. Snap the door on the plastic van back into place or superglue a doll back together. But now they bring me their iPhone or computer. Are you serious? I was relying on THEM to teach ME how to use it! Still, there is something inside of me that thinks, *I should be able to fix this. I should be able to do anything set before me.*

What's your list look like? Maybe it's a vacation packed with activities with no time to rest. Maybe it's a class load filled with hours you'll never be able to keep up with. Perhaps it's relational circles you can't fully satisfy. Jen Hatmaker, in her book *For the Love*, writes about the problem of imitating lives of people who seem to do everything as seen in social media:

> Here is part of the problem . . . No one constructed fairytale child-hoods for their spawn, developed an innate set of personal talents, fostered a stimulating and world-changing career, created stunning homes and yard-scapes, provided homemade food for every meal (locally sourced, of course), kept all marriage fires burning, sustained meaningful relationships in various environments, carved out plenty of time for "self care," served neighbors/church/world, and maintained a fulfilling, active relationship with Jesus our Lord and Savior. You can't balance that job description. Listen to me: No one can pull this off.[1]

There's another word for this: *omnipotence*. And yes, only God can do that.

Omnipotence refers to God's unlimited power, or as is commonly stated, God is "all-powerful." This kind of stems from the notion that God is Creator; God created the world and everything in it, and thus displays an awesome power that humans cannot even fathom. He is all-powerful.

When appearing to Abraham, then called Abram, God introduces himself as "Almighty":

> The Lord appeared to him and said, "I am God Almighty; walk before me faithfully and be blameless."
>
> Genesis 17:1

And in Job 11:7, Job's buddy Zophar replies to Job,

> "Can you fathom the mysteries of God? Can you probe the limits of the Almighty?"

In a sermon, pastor and author Kyle Idleman tells the story of his efforts one day to push a desk down the hallway. Midway through this process, his four-year-old son offered his assistance. Kyle thought this gesture was a sweet childlike effort of a son trying to be like his dad. But then his son said, "I got it, Dad. I don't need your help," and then began trying to push this big piece of furniture on his own. The desk didn't budge. But his son kept trying. Kyle said, "As he was straining to push this immovable object, I couldn't help but laugh. Not at my son, but at myself. This is exactly what I do to my heavenly Father."

Philosopher Søren Kierkegaard states

> Spiritual pride is the illusion that we are competent to run our own lives, achieve our own sense of self-worth and find a purpose big enough to give us meaning in life without God.[2]

Again, our question is, Can we let God be God . . . or do we feel the need to help him out?

The people of Israel declared they could do this on their own . . . and they sunk deeper into despair. Aren't you glad we learned from their mistake?!

A *New York Times* article reported that Yale University lists its most popular class ever as being PSYC 157: Psychology and the Good Life. Nearly 25 percent of all students at Yale registered for it. Laurie Santos, the psychology professor who teaches the course, and the head of one of Yale's residential colleges, "tries to teach students how to lead a happier, more satisfying life in the twice-weekly lectures." Interestingly,

> A 2013 report by the Yale College Council found that more than half of undergraduates sought mental health care from the university while enrolled. "In reality, a lot of us are anxious, stressed, unhappy, numb," said Alannah Maynez, 19, a freshman taking

the course. "The fact that a class like this has such large interest speaks to how tired students are of numbing their emotions—both positive and negative—so they can focus on their work, the next step, the next accomplishment."

One of Santos's principal eye-opening lessons is that

the things Yale undergraduates most associate with achieving happiness—a high grade, a prestigious internship, a good-paying job—do not increase happiness at all. "Scientists didn't realize this in the same way 10 or so years ago, that our intuitions about what will make us happy, like winning the lottery and getting a good grade—are totally wrong," Dr. Santos said.[3]

Could it be that all of our attempts to be God and do his job have led us to the same despair that the people of Israel felt? Though we may not be in physical exile and servitude like they experienced, we certainly know what it is like to be exiled in our loneliness and enslaved to our need to control.

Gallup released results of a survey of more than 2.5 million Americans regarding how people felt in their day-to-day lives—in other words, their "well-being." The overall results "show a nation where well-being is in sharp decline." In fact, 2017 reflected "the largest year-over-year decline in the 10-year history of the Well-Being Index."[4]

Maybe it's time we take Micah up on his suggestion.

What does it mean to let God be God, and we just be humble?

Walk Wisely

Dr. Jeremy Smoak says we can even take the word *humbly* to another level. He suggests that "walk humbly" might be better translated "walk wisely":

I would argue that the verb here actually connotes the importance of study and intellectualism. The wise study Torah and culture and discern how culture systematically disadvantages people and then kindness and justice represent the action of doing something to change this. I like "walk wisely" because it pairs action and intellect: intellect that walks.[5]

He would then translate this passage this way:

He told you, O man, what is good
    Yahweh wants nothing of you, except that you
    Do justice
    Love kindness
    And walk wisely with your God.

This lines up with how Eugene Peterson translated James 3:13–16 in *The Message*:

Do you want to be counted wise, to build a reputation for wisdom? Here's what you do: Live well, live wisely, live humbly. It's the way you live, not the way you talk, that counts. Mean-spirited ambition isn't wisdom. Boasting that you are wise isn't wisdom. Twisting the truth to make yourselves sound wise isn't wisdom. It's the furthest thing from wisdom—it's animal cunning, devilish conniving. Whenever you're trying to look better than others or get the better of others, things fall apart and everyone ends up at the others' throats.

James is reminding us that humility leads to wisdom. And wisdom leads to humility.

When my youngest daughter, Sidney, was around six, she brought some perspective and humility to my life in one swift sentence. We were tucking the kids into bed, and when we got to her room, I leaned over the bed and kissed her forehead. She looked at me and said what I thought to be "You have big muscles." Assuming she was eyeing my biceps that were displayed near her head, I was very flattered. I thought, *Well, I have been working out. If she's noticed, I'm sure others have as well.* I responded, "Oh, Daddy has big muscles! Thank you!" But just before I left the room to go order sleeveless shirts, she corrected me. "No, I said you have big nostrils." Suddenly I wasn't as flattered.

Paul seems to be bringing us down to size like this when he writes to the Corinthians:

> Instead, God chose things the world considers foolish in order to shame those who think they are wise. And he chose things that are powerless to shame those who are powerful. God chose things despised by the world; things counted as nothing at all, and used them to bring to nothing what the world considers important. As a result, no one can ever boast in the presence of God. God has united you with Christ Jesus. For our benefit God made him to be wisdom itself. Christ made us right with God; he made us pure and holy, and he freed us from sin. Therefore, as the Scriptures say, "If you want to boast, boast only about the Lord."
>
> 1 Corinthians 1:27–31 NLT

It's as if the greatest opponent to the power of the cross is not Satan, our failures, or our lack of knowledge, but rather our thinking that we have big muscles, when the reality is we just have a big nose.

How Jesus Did This

Besides his crucifixion and resurrection, the most significant event in the life of Jesus has to be the Last Supper. What goes on in that upper room is so significant, John spends nearly 25 percent of his biography about Jesus on this one evening.

It is significant from a theological standpoint. Up until this point, the Passover meal was done to remember God passing over the Israelites, bringing justice upon the Egyptians, and rescuing his people from slavery. But Jesus says, "After tonight . . . you will have this meal to remember me." God is going to pass over everyone by bringing justice upon me for your sin and thus rescue you from being enslaved to your sin. This was huge. And no one there knew it. Yet.

It is significant from a humility standpoint. Judas will get up and leave so he can go betray Jesus for a bag of money. Peter will argue with Jesus about his own level of dedication and loyalty. Several of the others will argue about which of them is the greatest. And Jesus will quietly get up, grab a towel and a basin of water, and begin washing their feet. While everyone else is taking a position of power, wealth, or authority, Jesus takes the position of a servant.

But it is also significant from a "how to follow me" standpoint. Jesus is about to rewrite the rule book for what it means to be good with God. In the beginning it started with one rule: Don't eat of the tree. #epicfail. Then it turned into ten rules: the Ten Commandments. The Israelites failed that one before Moses could even bring them down the mountain. After that, it was a colossal mess of breaking these and offering sacrifices for forgiveness. The Pharisees enacted over six hundred laws just to help us all keep the original ten. That was pretty overwhelming. And then Jesus comes around and reduces it to two.

> "Teacher, which is the greatest commandment in the law?" Jesus replied, "'Love the Lord your God with all your heart and with all your soul and with all your mind.' This is the first and greatest commandment. And the second is like it: 'Love your neighbor as yourself.' All the Law and the Prophets hang on these two commandments.'"
>
> Matthew 22:36–40

Love God. Love people. That seems more memorable than six hundred commands.

But in the upper room, at the Last Supper, Jesus makes it even easier. He says something so shocking and so stunning, I bet no one even moved:

> "A new command I give you . . ."
>
> John 13:34

Now, hold on! You can't make up new laws, can you? The disciples must have been thinking, *Sure, you can heal people. And I think you can even forgive people. But can you make up new commands? That seems like something only God can do.* Precisely. Here's what Jesus says:

> "Love one another. As I have loved you, so you must love one another."
>
> John 13:34

He reduces it all down to one thing: How you love people shows how you love God.

As a dad, I suppose I understand this. If you are complimentary to me but rude to my kids, then I don't care how much you liked the message—we are not good. It must be how our heavenly Father feels when we sing praises to him in church, then go out in the parking lot and call someone an idiot when they cut us off.

> **How you love people shows how you love God.**

Pastor Andy Stanley refers to this as "horizontal morality." For years we've lived with "vertical morality." Sacrifice to God, give to God, sing to God, study about God, talk about God . . . in other words, LOVE GOD. But we tend to LOVE PEOPLE when we are in a good mood around people who we naturally like. Jesus recalibrates the law by stating, "No more LOVE GOD / LOVE PEOPLE. Now it is LOVE PEOPLE . . . it's the way you show you LOVE GOD."

And this is exactly what Micah was calling us toward. Notice nothing he says is about how we love God . . . but all of it is to show we love God. Act justly, love mercy, walk humbly. These things not only put God back on the throne, but they live out Jesus' call on our lives.

Following Jesus isn't always easy, but it's not complicated: Justice. Mercy. Humility. Repeat.

A Simple Way to Follow

One of the things I find helpful is to look at people I know who I think live this out and see how they do it.

I think about the late musician Rich Mullins. Rich grew up in Indiana, made it big in the Christian music industry in the 1990s, and then disappeared to live in obscurity on an Indian reservation in Arizona, where he taught music to kids. He made millions but gave it all away. He never married, never had kids, and died at the age of forty-two in a car accident in the middle of the night in the middle of nowhere. Yet I will never forget him, and if you've ever heard his music, listened to an interview, or saw him perform, I bet you'll never forget him either. He was driven by his desire for justice for the oppressed, overcome by mercy for the forgotten, and possessed the humility of a self-proclaimed ragamuffin. Justice. Mercy. Humility. Repeat.

I take a look at my buddy Steve. I met Steve when he and I were both in seventh grade. We spent the next ten years going to school together, attending college, were even in each other's weddings—pretty much inseparable. We were two self-righteous, obnoxious teens/young adults who had enough sense to appear smart but not enough to be kind. In hindsight, we were probably both insensitive, racist, sexist, and arrogant. Oh, we loved God. It was the people who got in the way.

After college we went our separate ways to work in churches. And while I took my own path of self-discovery, trying to love God better, Steve took another path. He chose people. He poured his life into students—and not just the church kid, but the reckless, rebellious, "don't want to go to church if you paid me" kids. And he changed their lives. He traveled the world with mission trips and partnered with organizations to bring awareness to those in need. And when we met up again some ten years later, we were so different. He loved people, and thus God. My pursuits just left me wondering if God loved me. Clearly Steve chose the better path. I look at his life and think: Justice. Mercy. Humility. Repeat.

I look at my wife, Lorrie. If there is anyone who has impressed upon me the value of loving others, it is she. While being a fellow introvert who stays away from the spotlight, she quietly and faithfully practices small acts of mercy and kindness to many she meets and some who never have the pleasure. She is always speaking up for the overlooked. I can recall our going to a movie one night where we saw a college-age student from our church. She said, "I think he's alone. Let's ask him to sit with us." I'd like to say I welcomed the chance, but I was on a date night, so I was a bit reluctant. On other occasions I've seen her randomly pay for the vehicle behind us while we are in the drive-through at Chick-fil-A. Every night before Easter she takes the kids out and they secretly place eggs in the yards of every family on our street with kids young enough to care. And for years she operated a preschool in our home, granting discounts and scholarships to more families than I would have naturally thought of. Ask her if she's making a difference. Oh, no . . . just trying to be kind. Justice. Mercy. Humility. Repeat.

When I choose to repeat justice, mercy, and humility . . . it changes me.

It directs my attention to others who have it worse than I do.

It makes me aware of those who are overlooked and in need.

It causes my heart to break for those far from God.

It forces me to pick up trash on the street, open doors for people, let people in front of me in line, and not count the items in someone's cart if I'm in the express lane!

It convicts me to stop complaining about spotty cell service and cold pizza and start sponsoring more kids.

It gets me off of my soapbox about the need for people to use their turn signals and stop texting at the dinner table . . . and it makes me advocate for the poor and the enslaved.

It causes me to not take credit for what I didn't do.

I begin to be happy for someone who succeeds more than I do.

It makes me slow down, want to listen more, and seek to understand.

It makes me prioritize things that matter.

I stop saying, "I deserve this . . ."

I see the good things in my life as a privilege instead of a right.

It makes me sit down and invest in others.

I walk across the street and say hi.

I use my horn less.

I pay for the person behind me in the drive-through.

I stop complaining about everything and correcting everyone on social media.

I enjoy now . . . rather than living in the past or the future.

It reminds me I'm not the center of the universe.

And oddly enough, it looks a lot like Jesus, who, by the way, IS the center of the universe.

Justice. Mercy. Humility. Repeat.
It's not easy. But it's not complicated.

TO-DO LIST

- Pick three things from the list above and make them your goals for the next week.

DISCUSSION QUESTIONS

1. Who are examples in your life that you look at to show you Jesus?
2. What are their characteristics that you admire the most?
3. What items on the above list are the most difficult for you?

Acknowledgments

There are so many who make a book happen. To list them all would be longer than the book itself, so let me just mention a few. Thank you to my family for giving me the space to write. Lorrie, Lindsey, and Sidney, you're the best. And I love you. Thank you to Debbie Robert. Your patience, direction, and protection of my calendar and me allowed this to happen. Thank you to Mike Breaux. While I didn't get the tattoo, your passion for this verse became mine as well. Thank you to Steve Meyers, who introduced me to a bigger view of justice. Thank you to Josh Komo. Your research, assistance, and wisdom made my words make sense. Thank you to Brad Williams, HiHat Production, Brittany Bowling, Danny Caudillo, Don Gates, Andy McGuire, and all of the wonderful team at Bethany House. I stand on your shoulders.

Notes

Chapter 1 Why Is This So Complicated

1. "St. Simeon Stylites the Elder," New Advent, www.newadvent.org/cathen/13795a.htm.

2. Jennifer Egan, "Power Suffering," New York Times magazine, May 16, 1999, https://partners.nytimes.com/library/magazine/millennium/m2/egan.html.

3. 1 Corinthians 9:27, NASB (1977) translation.

4. Sara Malm, "Motor City's Messiah," Daily Mail, December 18, 2013, www.dailymail.co.uk/news/article-2525844/The-Jesus-guy-Bearded-man-familiar-sight-Jerusalem-wearing-robe-carrying-cross-revealed-Detroit-preacher.html.

5. Matthew 16:24

6. Matthew 5:45

Chapter 2 What Micah Learned in Sunday School

1. Lysa TerKeurst, What Happens When Women Walk in Faith: Trusting God Takes You to Amazing Places (Eugene, OR: Harvest House, 2005), 191.

Chapter 3 Your God May Not Be THE God

1. Bruce Wilkinson wrote the mega-seller The Prayer of Jabez, addressing Jabez's request for God to enlarge his territory (1 Chronicles 4:10).

2. "Americans Check Their Phones 80 Times a Day: Study," New York Post, November 8, 2017, https://nypost.com/2017/11/08/americans-check-their-phones-80-times-a-day-study/.

3. Beth Moore, Believing God Bible study (Nashville: B&H Publishing, 2004, 2015), 47–48.

Chapter 4 Who God Was to Micah, Jesus, and Now You

1. Carey Nieuwhof, Mark Clark on Apologetics for Post-Christian, Post-Modern Young Adults: Sex, Hell, Science and So Much More," CNLP: 151, July 31, 2017, https://careynieuwhof.com/episode151/.

Chapter 5 Leveraging the Full Power of God in Your Life

1. Fred Sanders, *The Deep Things of God* (Wheaton, IL: Crossway, 2017), 61.

Chapter 6 The Two Sides of Justice

1. Dr. Jeremy Smoak, email message to author.
2. Miroslav Volf, *Exclusion and Embrace: A Theological Exploration of Identity, Otherness, and Reconciliation* (Nashville: Abingdon, 1996), 215, emphasis added.
3. Miroslav Volf, *Exclusion and Embrace*, 216.
4. Christine Caine, *Undaunted* (Grand Rapids, MI: Zondervan, 212), 166.
5. Richard Rohr, "Finally Getting Over Your 'Self' with the Enneagram, pt. 1," Typology podcast, Episode 14, October 4, 2017, http://typology.libsyn.com/014_typology_richardrohr_final.

Chapter 7 When Helping Is Hurting

1. Steve Corbett and Brian Fikkert, *When Helping Hurts* (Chicago: Moody Publishers, 2009), 51.
2. Corbett and Fikkert, *When Helping Hurts*, 53.
3. Ronald Sider, *Just Generosity* (Grand Rapids, MI: Baker Books, 2007), 67.
4. Corbett and Fikkert, *When Helping Hurts*, 37–38.
5. Sider, *Just Generosity*, 70.
6. Sider, *Just Generosity*, 77.
7. Corbett and Fikkert, *When Helping Hurts*, 100–101.
8. Rodney Stark, *The Rise of Christianity* (Princeton, NJ: Princeton University Press, 1996), 155.
9. Stark, *The Rise of Christianity*, 166.

Chapter 8 Self-Justice

1. Dr. Tasha Eurich, "What Self-Awareness Really Is (and How to Cultivate It)," *Harvard Business Review*, January 4, 2018, https://hbr.org/2018/01/what-self-awareness-really-is-and-how-to-cultivate-it.
2. Mark Gignilliat, "What Does the Lord Require of You?" *Christianity Today*, November, 2017, 46–49.
3. Hannah Arendt, *Eichmann in Jerusalem: A Report on the Banality of Evil*, revised and enlarged edition (New York: Viking Press, 1964), 54.
4. Richard Beck, *Reviving Old Scratch: Demons and the Devil for Doubters and the Disenchanted* (Minneapolis: Fortress Press, 2016), 105.
5. Hannah Arendt, *The Life of the Mind* (New York: Harcourt Brace Jovanovich), 1978, n.p.

Chapter 9 For Those We Know and Love

1. Brené Brown, *Rising Strong* (New York: Spiegel and Grau, 2015), 9.

Chapter 10 For Those We Don't Know and Don't Love

1. David Wasserman, "Purple America has All But Disappeared," FiveThirtyEight, March 8, 2017, https://fivethirtyeight.com/features/purple-america-has-all-but-disappeared/.
2. Richard Beck in Rob Goetze, "With Arms Wide Open," Exclusion and Embrace, March 10, 2015, http://exclusionandembrace.blogspot.com/2015/03/moral-circles.html.
3. Andy Stanley, Drive Conference 2017.
4. Kristin Schell, *The Turquoise Table* (Nashville: Thomas Nelson, 2017).

Chapter 11 Receiving Mercy

1. Brown, *Rising Strong*, 194.
2. Timothy Keller, *The Freedom of Self-Forgetfulness* (Lancashire, England: 10Publishing, 2012), Kindle.
3. Keller, *The Freedom of Self-Forgetfulness*.
4. Brené Brown, "The Power of Vulnerability," TEDx Houston, June 2010, https://ted.com/talks/brene_brown_on_vulnerability.
5. Brown, *Rising Strong*, 50.

Chapter 12 When Confidence Becomes Pride

1. Jim Collins, *How the Mighty Fall* (New York: Collins Business Book, 2009), 20.
2. C.S. Lewis, *Mere Christianity* (New York: Macmillan Publishers, 1952).
3. Keller, *The Freedom of Self-Forgetfulness*.
4. Keller, *The Freedom of Self-Forgetfulness*.

Chapter 13 When Self-Deprecation Becomes a Sin

1. Samuel Chand, *Leadership Pain* (Nashville: Thomas Nelson, 2015), 178.
2. Keller, *The Freedom of Self-Forgetfulness*.

Chapter 14 Giving God His Job Back

1. Jen Hatmaker, *For the Love: Fighting for Grace in a World of Impossible Standards* (Nashville: Thomas Nelson, 2015), 4.
2. Søren Kierkegaard, *The Sickness unto Death* (Princeton, NJ: Princeton University Press, 1980).
3. David Shimer, "Yale's Most Popular Class Ever: Happiness," *New York Times*, January 26, 2018, https://www.nytimes.com/2018/01/26/nyregion/at-yale-class-on-happiness-draws-huge-crowd-laurie-santos.html.
4. Alyssa Davis, "Gallup's Top Well-Being Findings of 2017," Gallup, January 10, 2018, https://news.gallup.com/poll/224675/gallup-top-findings-2017.aspx.
5. Dr. Jeremy Smoak, personal email to the author.

Author's Note

Thank you for reading *Justice. Mercy. Humility*! Can I give you a free gift to say Thanks? Go to my website, pastorrustygeorge.com, and enter the promotional code JMH.

Thanks again!

About the Author

Rusty George is the lead pastor of Real Life Church (RLC) in Valencia, California. Over his fifteen years at RLC, the church has grown to more than 6,000 people and three campuses. Rusty speaks regularly at conferences across the country, and he lives with his wife and two daughters in Santa Clarita, California.

More Practical and Powerful Resources by Rusty George

Discover how to satisfy your deepest needs through the power of *us*. When we learn to live in true community, we connect with God better; heal better; and overcome fears, raise families, fight temptations, and bless the world around us better. Find the fulfillment you've been looking for, and see for yourself how God uses *we* to bring out the best in *me*.

Better Together